ENDORSEMENTS

Dr. Kay Daigle knows what she's talking about! In this excellent book exploring the six vital growth areas essential to effective leadership, she takes us deep while always anchoring the truths that might elude us to practical leadership examples drawn from personal ministry experience. She knows her subject matter and she knows women. She knows what it takes for a woman to move from "ordinary" to someone well prepared as a godly leader. Furthermore, she ends each chapter with an action program for personal assessment and growth. It is hard to imagine a more accessible, comprehensive and practical handbook for any woman who wants to be all that God created her to be.

Dr. Alice Mathews, teacher on the daily radio Bible class *Discover the Word*

From Ordinary Woman to Spiritual Leader is a book with which most women can not only identify but gain personal benefit. One of the things I appreciate about this project is that it compels the reader to personalize her own journey, chapter by chapter. This is a tool that could be used in any context—one-to-one or group—with the outcome being greater benefit to the local and global church. This book fills a great need—women whom God has gifted but who have yet to realize their place in the Kingdom. I not only recommend this book, I know I will be using it as I minister to women.

Dr. Beverly Hislop, author of *Shepherding a Woman's Heart* (Moody)
and *Shepherding Women in Pain* (Moody) www.shepherdingwomen.com

Drawing on extensive ministry experience, Kay Daigle traces her life from leader-in-training to trainer of leaders. In *From Ordinary Woman to Spiritual Leader* she offers a well-tested guide to recognizing one's leadership potential and developing characteristics necessary for high-quality influence. A great resource from someone who's "been there," this guide casts a vision for spiritual leadership that trains women to lead biblically. Readers who apply the principles in this book will be challenged, encouraged, and changed—and so will the people they serve.

Sandra Glahn, adjunct professor at Dallas Seminary
and author of the Coffee Cup Bible Study Series

This book is a very useful combination of biblical principles, quotes from other sources, and practical ideas from the author's own experiences in leading women. The thoughtful questions at the end of each chapter should help the reader to examine her own leadership style and make corrections where necessary. This is a valuable resource for anyone in a leadership role.

Vickie Kraft, author of *Women Mentoring Women* (Moody) and *The Influential Woman* (Thomas Nelson) and founder of Titus 2:4 Ministries

Too many women desire to lead for Jesus but let their fears and lack of training curb what God wants to do through them. Kay Daigle's *From Ordinary Woman to Spiritual Leader* walks potential female leaders step by step through the essentials: leading from a spiritual core, issues of character and calling, how to care and communicate, and how to develop competence. Dr. Daigle draws from her extensive experience as both a vocational minister and a lay volunteer to write an indispensable handbook for leery women contemplating leadership. Her book is well-written, honest, encouraging, and full of stories of surprised women like herself who discovered the leader within.

Dr. Sue Edwards, Associate Professor of Christian Education, Dallas Theological Seminary

Kay Daigle has written a thoughtful, Biblical and comprehensive book regarding leadership development in a woman's life. She covers all the bases, from a woman's personal spiritual journey to how one grows into a leader. The Personal Action Plan at the end of each chapter provides a framework for the reader to see how to practically apply the principles taught. Kay's own experience and the stories of women that are included illustrate how powerful these truths are and how crucial they are for women who truly desire to serve God in an extraordinary way.

Susie Hawkins, author of *From One Ministry Wife to Another* (Moody)

Kay Daigle writes with humble wisdom, leading us through the discovery of our God-given talents and into the place where we can employ them for glory of God's kingdom, and for our greatest joy. Honoring that which is most *ordinary*, she shows us the path to a life of *extraordinary* passion.

Jan Winebrenner, author of *Intimate Faith* (Warner) and *The Grace of Catastrophe* (Moody), JanWinebrenner.com

Many of us relate to Kay's surprise at God's call on her life to lead. When faced with such a surprising opportunity, this book gives "shoe leather" counsel for developing leadership skills. The practical Personal Action Plans stimulate the reader to accurately and honestly assess themselves so as to better follow the Lord and lead those she is called to serve. Add this to your library today.

Gwynne Johnson, Board Member, Entrust International. Author of Entrust curriculum, "Developing a Discerning Heart"

From

ORDINARY WOMAN
to Spiritual Leader

GROW YOUR INFLUENCE

By Kay Daigle

WestBow
PRESS
A DIVISION OF THOMAS NELSON

ISBN: 978-1-4497-6204-9 (sc)
ISBN: 978-1-4497-6205-6 (hc)
ISBN: 978-1-4497-6203-2 (e)
Library of Congress Control Number: 2012914177

WestBow Press books may be ordered through booksellers or by contacting:
WestBow Press
A Division of Thomas Nelson
1663 Liberty Drive
Bloomington, IN 47403
www.westbowpress.com
1-(866) 928-1240

Printed in the United States of America
WestBow Press rev. date: 9/06/2012

To my husband Gary,
For your continuous support and encouragement
to use my gifts to the utmost.
Without you, there would be no book.

TABLE OF CONTENTS

ACKNOWLEDGEMENTS

Because this book is built upon a lifetime of living and learning, countless people are part of my journey—too many to name. Those mentioned below represent a much larger group of people who invested in my personal growth as a spiritual leader.

Those who taught me the Bible, including my parents, Kay Arthur and her team at Precept Ministries, and my seminary professors, influenced me greatly. I appreciate their faithful study and love for God's Word.

Countless women modeled godly Christian leadership as they volunteered in small and large roles in the churches I attended. Their influence on my life has been extensive.

My understanding of serving as a female minister grew because of the supportive community and godly wisdom of Christy McFarland, Dianne Miller, Karin Benningfield, Liz Freethy, and Amanda Kruse who all worked with me long-term at Northwest Bible Church. Other women in ministry greatly encouraged me as we shared our journeys, particularly Susie Hawkins, Claudia McGuire and Michelle Attar. The cohort of women in my D.Min. program at Gordon-Conwell and our mentor Alice Mathews left a lasting imprint on my perspective of women in ministry. That community pictured the breadth of people in heaven, both in their various evangelical perspectives and their backgrounds.

I was also blessed to serve with some incredible male ministers at both Prestonwood Baptist Church and Northwest Bible Church who greatly contributed to my growth as a leader.

My prayer team faithfully prayed for me during the writing, publication, and editing of this book. My thanks go to Micki Maris, Suzy Bastian, Cathie Adams, Sharon Thomas, Susan Curry, Cindy Henderson, Mary Bomar, Bob Ann Talkington, Sarah Hilgart, Kay Halligan, D'Ann Riemer, Sarabeth Sanderson, and also to Evelyn Babcock and Irish Kinney, who not only prayed but helped revise and edit the manuscript. I appreciate the support of many other unnamed friends and family who encouraged and prayed for me long before I ever began to write this book.

I am indebted to those who read and endorsed this book—Alice Mathews, Vickie Kraft, Bev Hislop, Sue Edwards, Susie Hawkins, Jan Winebrenner, Sandi Glahn, and Gwynne Johnson. Despite their own busy lives, they graciously gave their time to me. Thank you, Gail Seidel, for providing input on the "Centered in Christ" essential. Alice, Susie, and Gwynne graciously sent the manuscript to their publishing connections. I appreciate the faith that all of you showed in this project.

This book would not be complete without the personal stories contributed so generously by various women whose names are scattered throughout the book. God will use their experiences to help the rest of us grow our own influence.

I am grateful to the volunteers who served alongside me when I was on staff at Prestonwood Baptist Church and Northwest Bible Church. Their support for my leadership and love for me were invaluable in my own journey.

INTRODUCTION

My Story

My own journey to spiritual leadership was not part of a plan or an ambition. From a human perspective it seems like I fell into it, somewhat kicking and screaming. I was simply an ordinary woman who wanted to stay that way. Having been disenchanted by spiritually proud Christians early in my life, I wanted to be somewhat incognito with my faith—taking my two children to church on Sunday and finding a few good friends within our congregation without making a fuss about it. But God had other plans.

The young women's group at our church proved to be a great place to meet other moms, and it offered unexpected benefits. Each month an older woman taught us from God's Word, challenging my thinking about very practical issues of life. At the same time, my husband and I attended a couples' class co-led by a woman, who was actually the first exceptional Bible teacher whom I had ever heard. Because of the spiritual leadership of these two women, the Scriptures began to come alive in my mind and heart, and God began to change me.

In time our tiny women's group faced a leadership crisis and needed someone to step up. Although God seemed to be tapping me on the shoulder as the group discussed it, I refrained from volunteering. If God wanted me to direct them, he would have to get them to ask. What a relief when one of the minister's wives volunteered! She requested my help, and I agreed; after all, the responsibility seemed minimal and wouldn't threaten my life of being ordinary in the least. Within months, however, her economic situation pushed her to accept a more demanding job position, and she turned it all over to me.

Now, I had often been a leader in school and college activities. It wasn't the leadership that bothered me; it was the spiritual aspect of it.

I wanted to please God, but only if I could remain a normal, ordinary woman instead of considering myself better than others, as too many Christians whom I had observed imagined themselves. Yet the women who were leading me at this church were passionate about Jesus without being proud. They were encouraging and loving without condemning or criticizing. God began to take my fears and replace them with faith in him, and I dared to lead.

When we moved a few months later, I knew that I needed to find another group focused on the Bible. God's Word was changing me as I entrusted him with life issues. I learned that our new church had a women's small group Bible study in our neighborhood. There I met some great Christian women who became close friends and encouragers. The study challenged me to really dig into the Scriptures. I loved spending time wrestling with them personally each week.

As a bonus, our new couples' class at church featured an outstanding teacher who continued to build on the biblical foundation from my childhood. As he led us through 1 Corinthians, he talked about spiritual gifts; I had never heard of them despite my years in church. How exciting that God had gifted an ordinary woman like me! His Spirit was there to give me power and produce fruit when I served in my area of giftedness, but I was clueless about the identity of my gifts. Our teacher suggested that our desires would help us discover them, but my only desire was to teach knowledgably and fervently, as our previous teacher had always done with such excellence. How could I possibly do that? That would truly involve spiritual leadership, and I didn't feel at all qualified. I knew myself; how could God allow me to teach his Word? I was petrified of getting up in front of people and disliked sharing about myself. I was an ordinary woman who could never live up to the expectations.

Yet, because I was excited at the prospect of discovering my spiritual gifts, one night I said a prayer asking God to present me with an opportunity to teach, if that was indeed my gift. Early the next morning I woke to a frantic call from our leader, saying that she was terribly sick and would be unable to facilitate the group that day. She wondered if I would do it.

Despite my reluctance to be a spiritual leader, I recognized God's sovereign hand revealing his gifting and guidance to me as he thrust me into a new role. From that time forward, he continued to open doors of leadership for me in surprising ways. I never asked for a role or position; others always approached me. When an opportunity intersected with my gifts and the burdens of my heart, I stepped up, believing that God was in it. I continually sought education and training to help me fulfill my responsibilities well.

For more than thirty years, this journey has taken me to unexpected places of spiritual leadership. Despite directing entire ministries as a church staff member, I have never lost the perspective that I am an ordinary woman. However, now I know from experience that our God can take an ordinary woman and transform her into a spiritual leader.

Your Story

You are on your own personal journey with God who has a purpose and plan for you, just as he did for me. Your story may involve God-given opportunities to call groups to catch a vision of Christ's kingdom in their lives or through their ministries, as mine has. Your calling may consist of one-on-one spiritual encouragement for a co-worker or a child. Leadership is not simply about guiding organizations or committees, but it is also about inspiring people to grow more like Jesus. God wants all of us to intentionally influence those already in our lives—our children, friends, co-workers, and neighbors. As Christian women, we need to see every relationship as a place of potential leadership and every woman as a leader-in-the-making. It is your choice as to whether to take those God-given opportunities and lead spiritually. You are writing your own story as you walk with God and influence others. What legacy do you want to leave behind?

This can be the time to develop yourself and your influence, whether that affects one or many. Take the fundamentals of leadership, grow in them, and increase your spiritual influence. God is in the business of transforming ordinary women into spiritual leaders, and you are on his list. If you discern his voice and dare to follow it, someday you will hear him say, "Well done, my good and faithful servant!"

Chapter 1

The Fragrance of Leadership

What's in a name? That which we call a rose
By any other name would smell as sweet.
                          Romeo and Juliet (II, ii, 43 - 44)

As Juliet so wisely stated, it's not the name that determines the beauty and fragrance of the flower. We can recognize a rose simply by its unique scent. Is that true of leadership? Can we identify a leader without a title or position? If someone acts like a leader and smells like a leader, is she a leader even without the label?

What about you personally? Do you consider yourself a leader? Do you influence someone? If so, what would it take to turn that relationship into leadership? In other words, what is the fragrance of a leader?

Just last week, I discussed leadership concepts with a friend. When she heard the topic, she suggested that it wouldn't apply to her since she is not a leader. I disagree with her assessment, knowing that she encourages her children and grandchildren toward God's kingdom and inspires others to grow in faith through the Christian books that she has written. What is it that makes us feel that we aren't leaders unless we lead a committee, large ministry, or church? Why do we think that leadership requires an organized effort? What is the fragrance of leadership? Does my friend misunderstand its scent?

In her book 5 *Leadership Essentials for Women*, Linda Clark encourages women to recognize themselves as leaders: "God has a plan for every woman. If she is open to His guidance, she will discover the blessings of being a leader in ways that are unique to her."[1]

God has a unique plan for you that utilizes your personality, gifting, and life situation to intentionally influence others. It may be time to take that truth seriously and open your heart to follow him on a journey to fulfill his purposes. You have every reason to be excited about what God has in store for you as a leader.

I was an unwilling leader who found herself unexpectedly directing a team without a title on two different occasions. The first situation was not the designated chairperson's fault, but the second one was. The woman abandoned her responsibilities; she failed to take action or move the group forward toward its goal. Because of my natural tendency to get things done, I began to do much of her work. (Or perhaps, I just couldn't stand the feeling of having no one in control.) Although she continued to chair our meetings, she neglected her other duties. My response wasn't particularly positive toward her because I felt used. This wasn't delegation but abdication.

Who was the leader of that group? Was it the woman who held the title? The way we define the term leader will help us determine the answer to that question.

There are hundreds, likely thousands, of definitions of what it means to be a leader. Let's look at some of them. As we do, read them carefully, comparing them with one another. We can only recognize a leader by catching her scent.

- Unknown: "One who knows the way, goes the way, and shows the way"[2]
- Dwight D. Eisenhower: "Leadership is the art of getting someone else to do something you want done because he wants to do it."[3]
- Ted Engstrom: "Leadership is the ability to make things happen."[4]
- J. Oswald Sanders: "Leadership is influence, the ability of one person to influence others to follow his or her lead."[5]
- Fred Smith: "Leadership is getting people to work for you when they are not obligated." [6]
- J. Robert Clinton and Richard W. Clinton: "A leader is a person with a God-given capacity and a God-given responsibility who is influencing a specific group of God's people toward God's purposes for the group."[7]
- Garry Wills: "Leadership is mobilizing others toward a goal shared by the leader and followers."[8]
- George Barna: "A Christian leader is someone who is called by God to lead; leads with and through Christlike character; and

demonstrates the functional competencies that permit effective leadership to take place."[9]

Which elements mentioned in the various quotes are essential to the fragrance of leadership? Review the list and underline them. Which quote(s) do you like best? Go back and mark your favorites.

What about the typical leadership role? Does it fit your chosen description? Consider the situation where I functioned without a title or position. Who led that group according to the definition you chose?

Ponder the following scenario as you contemplate the elements of leadership. One of my spiritual gifts is teaching. Assume that is the sum total of my calling; in that case God's chief plan and purpose for me would be to teach his Word to others. According to some of these definitions, I would not be a leader because people would not work for me or accomplish a measurable goal with me. But if I influence them through my teaching to become more like Christ and to live out his kingdom in their lives and in the greater world, am I not a leader? What if I influence just one person to follow Jesus more closely? Which quotes would classify me as a leader?

Here is my definition, at least for the present. (However, I reserve the right to continue modifying it as I grow and learn.) *A leader serves others by influencing them to invest in a vision, following her lead to accomplish it.*

This particular explanation encompasses my teaching gift. Generally when I teach, I cast the following vision one way or another: you can affect your world as God transforms you from an ordinary person into one who looks like Jesus. If women grasp this concept, investing in achieving it through time with God, his Word, and his people, haven't I led them? After all, Jesus used his teaching to paint a picture of God's kingdom and thereby changed the world.

Certainly, those with titles and positions are easily recognized as leaders. My friend D'Ann chairs a Christmas luncheon committee which plans, organizes, and presents an outreach event so that women experience the love of Jesus. Many of my friends facilitate small groups that encourage other women in the Scriptures. Christy leads in a ministry that networks Christians who provide healthcare to the poor in urban and rural communities. In her church staff position, Amanda plans and organizes the Sunday morning children's ministry, leading a huge number of volunteers. Such roles involve both name and responsibility; they have the aroma of leadership. When there is no title or position and the work is less structured, we are less likely to term it leadership.

That is why I invite you to write your own definition of a leader. You can make it more specific to the spiritual or keep it broad as I did. Feel free to use words or phrases borrowed from others; after all, you aren't writing this for publication but to clarify your own understanding of the true fragrance of leadership.

What is necessary to be a leader? Write your thoughts and definition here:

Begin with the Fragrance of Jesus

In light of our interaction with various definitions, let's return to some of our original questions. Are you a leader? Do you influence someone? What would it take to turn that relationship into spiritual leadership?

Second Corinthians 2:14-16 says,

> But thanks be to God who always leads us in triumphal procession in Christ and who makes known through us the fragrance that consists of the knowledge of him in every place. For we are a sweet aroma of Christ to God among those who are being saved and among those who are perishing—to the latter an odor from death to death, but to the former a fragrance from life to life. And who is adequate for these things?

Intentionally or unintentionally, we are steering others spiritually, either toward Christ or away from him. Wherever we go, we, hopefully, leave behind his scent, thus opening up opportunities for us to draw people toward God's vision. The fragrance of Christ comes through our words, actions, and attitudes. Paul says that some are drawn to the fragrance while others are repelled by it. When we verbally communicate God's vision to those who enjoy the aroma so that they embrace it as their own, we lead them spiritually. The opportunity is there with our children, friends, co-workers, and extended families because our influence pervades every relationship that we have.

Leadership expert John Maxwell concurs, "The true measure of leadership is influence—nothing more, nothing less."[10]

What turns a relationship of influence into spiritual leadership? My answer is intentional spiritual communication. Once we determine to cast a vision for God's best and someone responds, we are guiding spiritually. We may begin by sharing our lives so that others whiff a trace of Jesus; eventually, however, we speak about our faith. The vision we cast may depict a need to follow Jesus for the friend seeking answers; it may paint a portrait of increased dependency on Christ for the struggling believer; or it may explain the future promise of bodily resurrection for someone with chronic illness. That's when the fragrance of Christ mixes with the fragrance of leadership, with or without the name.

Caye Cook shares her tribute to the wonderful woman who had a great effect on her life. Sis may not traditionally be identified as a leader, but her influence was intentional, spiritual, and long-lasting. I call that a leader.

> Sis came to work for our family when I was an infant. With twins, my mother needed help. Sis became part of the unshakeable framework in the home that dispensed law and order, carried the moral standard of ethics and behavior, and then slathered it all with love and chicken and dumplings. She became an integral part of our family and of what I thought of as home.

> I cannot think of a cruel word that she ever spoke to any of us. I cannot think of a bitter tone or unpleasant attitude towards me or any family member. I only remember her constant love and indomitable spirit.

> I cannot put into a few words or even several thousand the impact of Sis's life upon mine. It's impossible to distill a vibrant, well-lived life into something as measurable as letters on paper. All I know is that I loved her dearly and will miss her terribly. I will miss her effusiveness and her constant commentary on life. I will miss being deemed worthy to be entrusted with her thoughts. I will miss her strong voice and her endless, colorful expressions. I will miss being bragged on when she would say, "She's one of mine, one of my babies," beaming with the joy and satisfaction of love given and returned. I will miss her mockingbird song of love constantly chattered into my soul.

Sis lived each day exuding a confidence that came from a faith in God with deeper roots than I will ever have. I learned more about God through Sis' life than I did at seminary. Like St. Paul, Sis was not defeated by hardship, but stood tall as "more than a conqueror through Him that loved us." [11]

You are Called to Lead

Jesus calls all of his followers, just as he did Sis, to some form of spiritual leadership. Not all will head up ministries or committees; most of us will never pastor a church or evangelize thousands like Billy Graham. But the summons is still there, and God has put others in our path so that we help move them toward his kingdom.

We see this in Jesus's final charge to his followers, popularly labeled the Great Commission: "Then Jesus came up and said to them, 'All authority in heaven and on earth has been given to me. Therefore go and make disciples of all nations, baptizing them in the name of the Father and the Son and the Holy Spirit, teaching them to obey everything I have commanded you. And remember, I am with you always, to the end of the age.'" (Matt. 28:18-20).

Although only the disciples who walked with Jesus during his earthly ministry were with him on this occasion, the command applies to all believers, all who trust in him. He charged us to bring others to faith and then pass on his teaching to new disciples. The very future of the church is bound up in the need for every generation of Christians to fulfill Jesus's instructions.

The Great Commission calls each of us into spiritual leadership. You and I are accountable; we are the only Christians who influence specific people. We can either ignore our responsibility, or we can intentionally turn our influence into spiritual leadership. Every Christ-follower is his ambassador to the world and a model and teacher for believers who are younger in faith.

There is another call to leadership specifically for women. Titus 2:3-5 directs us to invest in the lives of younger women, a more specific instruction for teaching disciples. Fulfilling that responsibility may take the form of mentoring, teaching, or friendship. Being on a church staff, I often mentored seminary interns; but more often, I developed casual friendships with younger women with whom I connected well. Certainly, my teaching ministry has given me opportunities to spiritually invest in a larger group, but I would be a leader even if I only enjoyed the one-on-one situations. Women of faith are to call out faith in younger women.

God also requires some of us to lead through our spiritual gifts. Not all gifts involve leadership, but many do. If your particular gift set requires you to intentionally lead others spiritually, you must recognize your responsibility to do so. "Just as each one has received a gift, use it to serve one another as good stewards of the varied grace of God. Whoever speaks, let it be with God's words. Whoever serves, do so with the strength that God supplies, so that in everything God will be glorified through Jesus Christ. To him belong the glory and the power forever and ever. Amen," (1 Peter 4:10-11). Peter doesn't list specific gifts here, but he says that every believer is a steward; we don't own our gifts but are simply using what belongs to God. Some of us have abilities that require leadership; to be faithful, we must use them for God's glory.

One of the spiritual gifts with which God has graced me is leadership. As you know from reading my story in the introduction, that was not my idea or my ambition. It was God's plan, and he clearly has a sense of humor. If I leave that gift dormant, failing to grow it and rarely employing it to serve God's people, I will have to account for my neglect to God someday.

Certainly, those of us who are mothers are responsible to invest in the spiritual growth of our children. I love the way that Paul acknowledged the role of Timothy's mother and grandmother in his faith when he wrote his young protégé: "I recall your sincere faith that was alive first in your grandmother Lois and in your mother Eunice, and I am sure is in you. . . You know who taught you and how from infancy you have known the holy writings, which are able to give you wisdom for salvation through faith in Christ Jesus" (2 Tim. 1:5; 3:14-15).

God summons all believing women to affect the world by sharing the gospel and teaching Jesus' commands to others, including younger women and our children. In addition, God gives some of us specific spiritual gifts that require us to be leaders as well. All of these actions have the fragrance of leadership, whether or not they involve titles, positions, or power.

Jack Hayford shares his perspective of leadership: "Leading is something we all do. Every one of us has some kind of leadership role, although the scope of influence and the number of observer-followers varies widely."[12]

It's time to accept your influence as a form of leadership and invest in growing as a leader.

Enhance your Leadership Fragrance

What's in a name? Nothing—it doesn't matter if anyone else would call you a leader or whether you have a recognized position or title. You have the potential to grow and develop spiritual leadership skills, thereby influencing those around you. The decision and the determination to act are up to you.

Maxwell encourages everyone to grow as leaders: "Most people fail to recognize the value of leadership. They believe that leadership is only for a few . . . . They have no idea of the opportunities they're passing up when they don't learn to lead." [13]

Chris Brady puts it this way:

> The reality, however, is that all of us are called upon to lead at some point, and actually many points, in our lives. Everyone must lead sooner or later. The question really isn't whether or not one is a leader, but rather, when the time for leadership is required, will the person be ready? People lead in large and small ways throughout their lives. Most, however, aren't realizing the impact they are having and don't equip themselves as they should. [14]

If you are breathing, this subject is for you.

But you may say, "I am not prepared or ready to lead anyone else until I _____." Our inadequacy is a call to stretch ourselves in dependence on God, not to avoid responsibility.

J. Oswald Sanders comments about our tendency to excuse ourselves: "When God calls us, we cannot refuse from a sense of inadequacy. Nobody is worthy of such trust. When Moses tried that excuse, God became angry (Exodus 4:14). Let us not pass the buck of leadership because we think ourselves incapable."[15]

Each fundamental outlined in this book is necessary if you are to become the spiritual leader God has designed you to be. Yet, growing in them involves a lifetime; it is the journey of leadership. These aren't strengths and weaknesses that we can delegate, such as structuring an organization or writing or dealing with finances, but each is essential in your development as a spiritual leader by the power and grace of God. Since leading even one person requires employing every fundamental, improvement in every area will strengthen your influence.

Growing as a leader involves more than simply reading a book. Research reveals three requirements for leadership development:

+ Assessment—you must know who you are, where you are, your strengths and your weaknesses.
+ Challenge—you must actually try things that stretch you.
+ Support—you must have a community to come alongside you to encourage and reinforce your efforts. [16]

The Personal Action Plans that follow each chapter include all three of these conditions for developing your leadership, but they will be effective only if you choose to implement them.

Again, Sanders gives wise words: "Every Christian is obligated to be the best he can be for God. Like any other worthwhile activity, if leadership can be improved, we should seek to improve it. In so doing, we prepare ourselves for higher service that may be just around the next corner, though unseen at the present."[17]

I decided to go to seminary for that reason—to improve as a teacher of God's Word. I had no ambition to work for a church or to increase numbers in my Bible study classes. I simply desired to do my very best for God. When I had only one semester left in my studies, my pastor called me into his office and offered me a position on staff as Director of the Women's Ministry. As the ministers there sought to replace the previous director, they looked for a woman proven faithful in ministry and equipped by training. God opened a door of higher service, far beyond what I ever expected or aspired to do. Without seeing the road ahead, I had unknowingly prepared for it by choosing to grow.

Leadership is more about your heart than your skills, more about who you are than what you do. After all, that is how God identifies a leader: "God does not view things the way men do. People look on the outward appearance, but the Lord looks at the heart." (1 Sam. 16:7).

You already carry the fragrance of Jesus. Will you intentionally use it to influence others toward living out his kingdom?

Personal Action Plan

Chapter 1: The Fragrance of Leadership

> The first step toward improvement is to recognize weaknesses, make corrections, and cultivate strengths.[18]
>
> J. Oswald Sanders

Assessment
Reread Matthew 28:18-20.
Spend time before God considering how you are fulfilling the first part of this commandment. Where are you making disciples of Jesus? Have you ever taken a trip to share the good news about Jesus? If not, why not? Are you influencing people at work, in your neighborhood or within your own family? Rate yourself on a scale of 1-10, with 10 meaning consistently sharing the gospel both in your own world and out in the larger world. Give reasons for your rating.

Now review Titus 2:3-5 prayerfully in light of the second part of the Great Commission, to teach new disciples all that Jesus commanded. In what younger woman's life (either in age or faith) are you presently investing? Is she outside of your own family? Not all women have mature believers in their own families, and so they need you. God wants you to be an influence beyond your own children and grandchildren. Again, rate yourself from 1-10, with 10 meaning there is a younger believer outside your family with whom you are intentionally and consistently investing your life. Write down why you rated yourself as you did.

Over what people do you have influence? They may be in your family, your neighborhood, your business, or your circle of friends. Have you intentionally built into their lives spiritually in order to help them move toward the kingdom of God in their own hearts and lives? If not, why? Rate yourself again from 1-10, with 10 meaning consistent spiritual influence in your relationships.

Reread 1 Peter 4:10-11. We will study our gifts later so if you are unfamiliar with them, just skip this for now. If not, assess your faithfulness in using any gift that you have that necessitates leadership. (Not all do.) Again, rate yourself on a 1-10 scale, with 10 meaning presently and consistently using that gift.

Challenge

Spend time in prayer taking the results of your assessment before God. Note your lowest ratings. How can you specifically begin to make disciples? How will you search for opportunities to befriend younger women in order to encourage and teach them? (You can do this in many ways, such as an intergenerational small group, mentoring, or a mission opportunity.) How can you be more intentional in leading your own children to become disciples of Jesus? What can you do to develop or use a spiritual gift? Write down one specific thing you will do right now, or consider writing a goal for each area.

Support

Each fundamental that we cover requires Christian community for maximum development. One option for support is an accountability and prayer partner for this book. Another is to share your journey with a small group to which you belong. Ask God to direct you to the right supportive and encouraging community. If you prefer finding another woman, ask God to point you to someone more mature in the faith or someone in a leadership role. Give her the specifics of your plan this week and ask for prayer. See where you can support her growth, or read and work through this book together. Approach someone this week either for ongoing support or to pray for you in regard to this week's plan. Write down your thoughts.

Summary of my Plan:

My challenge(s):

My support in reaching this challenge:

CHAPTER 2

STRENGTHENING YOUR CORE
CENTERED IN CHRIST

> We can all lead others only as far along the road as we ourselves have traveled. Merely pointing the way is not enough. If we are not walking, then no one can be following, and we are not leading anyone.[19]
>
> J. Oswald Sanders

I hate to admit it, but I don't like to work out. It's boring, becomes redundant, and often seems pointless. Too often I have labored at the gym with so little obvious benefit that I gave up entirely. At one point, knowing that I desperately needed physical activity after sitting so much at a computer and in meetings, I hired a trainer to coach me. One of the areas that she forced me to exercise was my core. I had no clue that I needed to worry about that part of my body. Because it seemed fine to me, I researched it, hoping to eliminate that part of my workout. I learned that the core is where all body movement originates. When it is weak, there is little strength in the lower back and spine, leading to possible pain and injury. A strong core is essential to physical health.

In much the same way, our spiritual health is based upon our ongoing love relationship with Christ. That is the spiritual core of our lives; if we fail to keep it strong, we will not have the power to lead others well. As Sanders says, we cannot take anyone where we haven't gone ourselves.

This truth cannot be any clearer biblically. When asked which commandment is the greatest, Jesus answered, "Love the Lord your God with all your heart, with all your soul, with all your mind, and with all your strength" (Mark 12:30). Thank God that he doesn't accept us based on how well we do in this most vital area, but it is the crux of our spirituality—loving God. Strengthening the spiritual core means centering our lives in that love relationship and finding our ultimate significance in God's great love for us. It's all about him, not us.

Raised in a legalistic environment, I assumed that my outward righteousness made me more spiritual. There seemed to be unwritten lists of rules that determined who made the grade as a "good Christian." (Of course, the lists consisted only of activities that were not weaknesses for the lists' creators.) These guidelines were easier to obey than loving God wholeheartedly. Issues of the heart were unimportant—only behavior mattered.

When the immoral woman anointed Jesus, he taught his host about the connection between grace and love: "Her sins, which were many, are forgiven, thus she loved much; but the one who is forgiven little loves little" (Luke 7:47). It's ironic that the more we follow our own legalistic rules, thinking they make us spiritual, the less we love Christ because we aren't overwhelmed by his grace. It is only as we recognize our own shortcomings and need for mercy that we truly fall in love with him.

Thus, it's no surprise that when I found it impossible to keep my legalistic list, I began to love Jesus. That he uses me to lead others continues to overwhelm me and draw me closer to him as I recognize my sins of both the past and present. Thus, I have found it important to assess my relationship with him honestly and often.

Getting a Spiritual Check-up

My physical trainer performed a series of tests and measured all sorts of body parts to assess my fitness. (It was utterly embarrassing to me for her to know the truth.) She also asked me to keep a log of everything I ate and drank so that we could improve that as well. Not surprisingly, I really preferred keeping all of that information to myself so that I could continue eating as I pleased, even though it wasn't good for me.

Similarly, if you and I desire to love God and to produce spiritual fruit, even to intentionally influence others toward Christ, we need spiritual check-ups in much the same way. We must ask questions such as these: How strong is my love relationship with Christ? How much am I motivated by self rather than God? Am I seeking God's kingdom or my own will? All too often we don't want to admit our failures to anyone, even ourselves, because it is embarrassing. However, we cannot work on a problem unless it's identified.

My own spiritual check-ups have revealed areas of spiritual laziness. Sometimes I rely upon the power of Scripture to carry me through as a Bible teacher instead of concentrating on my own walk with Christ. Time and again I am too busy doing God's work to spend quality time with him. Far too frequently my prayers are more focused on my will than on God's. Instead of being energized by the Spirit, I often choose to do it myself, much as a two-year-old child insists on attempting things she isn't capable of handling. I have come to realize that I regularly need such assessments to alert me to these tendencies.

Jesus is clear: "Remain in me, and I will remain in you. Just as the branch cannot bear fruit by itself, unless it remains in the vine, so neither can you unless you remain in me. I am the vine; you are the branches. The one who remains in me—and I in him—bears much fruit, because apart from me you can accomplish nothing" (John 15:4-5).

Although I have never had a vineyard, we did own a beautiful peach tree in our side yard for a decade. Each March it budded, producing delicious peaches by July. Because our spring weather is unpredictable and frequently stormy, sometimes branches ended up on the ground, broken from the tree. Never once did those branches produce peaches! Likewise, I certainly won't bear spiritual fruit when I am disconnected from the source of my life, Jesus, who lived in total dependence on God himself. He said, "I can do nothing on my own initiative. Just as I hear, I judge, and my judgment is just, because I do not seek my own will, but the will of the one who sent me" (John 5:30). If Jesus, the God-man, relied on the Father while he walked the earth, how much more important is it for us to do the same thing?

Yet somehow we don't grasp this; we fool ourselves into thinking that we are spiritually healthy because we say a few words to God each morning, basically giving him orders for the day as if he were our servant. Certainly we go to church and connect with him there, at least when we aren't thinking about the week ahead or what we'll have for lunch. However, it is impossible for religious activities to draw us closer to God and impart his life into us when our hearts and minds are so far from him.

We lose connection with God without focused attention. When our own talking fills all of our time with him, there is no communion or real conversation. No wonder our relationships with God often seem empty and lifeless! For years all I knew about prayer was to petition my requests.

I failed to understand that I was centered on myself rather than God and his will.

Jesus was completely sold out to the Father's will, with the ultimate example occurring the night before his crucifixion: "Going a little farther, he threw himself down with his face to the ground and prayed, 'My Father, if possible, let this cup pass from me! Yet not what I will, but what you will'" (Matt. 26:39).

Instead of being committed to the Father's will and his glory, we often seek our own. We may even pursue places of leadership to find our own fulfillment. We hunt for acclaim, power, or praise of others. Yet quite often we fool even ourselves into believing that we are selfless and even sacrificial in our works. Do our hearts really echo Jesus' words—not my will but what you will? Do we truly desire Christ above all else?

Many years ago to my dismay, I discovered that my own pastor was full of himself rather than God. Lacking a women's minister, our team of volunteers sat down with him for input. Strangely, the conversation ended up focused on him. He informed us of his success in reaching people and growing a church, contrasting his many accomplishments to those of other pastors. God was barely mentioned and certainly received no credit. As I sat there, I became increasingly alarmed for the church and for this man. In this case pride did go before a fall; in time, the pastor fell hard. Although his church was large, most attendees were spiritual babies who followed a leader who wasn't centered in Christ. He was unable to take them where he had not gone himself.

Exercising the Core

To avoid fruitlessness, we must turn our hearts to Christ, centering who we are and what we do in him. We must not seek and serve God out of duty—checking off "quiet time" and "service" on our mental to-do lists. (I have certainly been guilty of this.) Spending time with God and serving others are good things, but our hearts can be far away from God despite outward appearances.

Do we just abandon time with God unless our hearts are in it? No, but it may help to change the look of those moments. Just as my physical workouts need variety to avoid boredom and to exercise every part of my body, my spiritual exercises must include a range of activities. I can't just repeat the same things over and over with God and expect them to become life-giving; I must modify my interaction with him when it grows lifeless.

Although time with God should express our uniqueness (some of us love to sing praise songs, and some of us prefer digging into his Word), we must also incorporate practices that stretch us and develop us where we are weak, pursuing disciplines that will cultivate the likeness of Jesus in us.

Christians through the centuries have practiced ways of connecting closely with God. Such practices are called spiritual disciplines because they involve training that builds the spirit, much as physical training does our bodies. As Jeff Iorg explains, "Discipline is doing what is best, not what is easiest. You are disciplined when you choose to do difficult things and make them a habit."[20] The key is in the commitment to prioritize space in your life to connect with God.

Jesus modeled spiritual disciplines. His teaching evidenced his study and memorization of scripture. The Gospels describe him escaping the crowds for solitude and silence to pray and hear from God. He followed the law, which required keeping Sabbath and fasting. He spent his life in simplicity and service. If Jesus prioritized such practices, shouldn't we? If he who is God left space for the Father in his life, can we do any less?

The excuse that I hear most often from those who aren't experiencing intimacy with God is that they don't have the time. I think Sanders has it right when he defines the real issue, "Our problem is not too little time, but making better use of the time we have. Each of us has as much time as anyone else."[21] Instead of giving ourselves excuses, we must honestly admit our failure to discipline our time to meet with God and take practical steps to carve out space to pursue our relationships with him.

Many wonderful books define a large variety of spiritual disciplines.[22] You might take the time to research them yourself. The following summaries of common practices are those which I have personally experienced as spiritually invigorating. Although you may have benefited from many of them, it may be profitable to recommit to some, grow in others, or incorporate new ones into your regular routine.

Prayer: Conversation with God

> Prayer is nothing more than an ongoing and growing love relationship with God the Father, Son, and Holy Spirit.[23]
> Richard J. Foster

Prayer is an indispensable habit for connecting with God. Jesus modeled the necessity for prayer in his own life, and repeatedly the Scriptures call us to pray. Nevertheless, I experienced years of struggle with this essential practice. Foster describes my problem: "Real prayer comes not from gritting our teeth but from falling in love."[24] Until I truly fell in love with God, I had to force myself to pray, knowing I was supposed to do so.

If you battle to prioritize prayer, ask God to grace you with more love for him. Ask him to give you the desire to know him and spend time with him. Reflect on your sin and the mercy in God's forgiveness. 1 John 4:19 says, "We love because he loved us first." Bask in that love so that you long to be with the one you love.

If you already enjoy a love relationship with God and a healthy prayer life, consider ways to mature in prayer. If you are inconsistent, commit to a reasonable amount of time at a doable hour of the day and then expand your time. Remember that Jesus had to teach the disciples to pray (Luke 11:1-4), and we, too, must develop this vital area of spiritual life.

Here are some ideas for growing in this practice:

- Study the lives of those who prayed, both in Scripture and in biographies.
- Study the prayers of the Bible and learn from their patterns.
- Increase your time in thanksgiving and praise.
- Regularly spend time in honest confession, followed by basking in the warmth of God's forgiveness.
- Pray scriptures.
- Focus your prayers on God's kingdom purposes in every circumstance (God's agenda and not your own).
- Pray liturgical prayers from sources such as *The Book of Common Prayer.*

Because I am easily distracted, I have discovered ways to focus in prayer. I pause to grow quiet and still before God, waiting until my mind is centered on him. I write out my words, enabling better concentration and making it easy to return to my train of thought when sidetracked. You may try speaking aloud to God if the situation permits.

God is teaching me to align my prayers with his will. That requires more listening and less talking, as well as a real desire for God's purposes to be accomplished. Just as children reveal their immaturity when they make everything in life about them, our spiritual immaturity is marked by how much our prayers center on us and our desires. Jesus tells us to pray for God's kingdom to come (Matthew 6:10). Praying scriptures for people and circumstances so that there are kingdom results is a way to grow as pray-ers.[25]

Treat prayer as time with a friend, in this case God—talking, listening, and simply enjoying his presence. Once you experience the value of intimacy with him, you will find your life empty in its absence.

Solitude and Silence

> Solitude is a place. It is a place and time that is set apart for God and God alone, a time when we unplug and withdraw from the noise of interpersonal interactions, from the noise, busyness and constant stimulation associated with life in the company of others. . . Silence deepens our experience of solitude, because in silence we choose to unplug not only from the constant stimulation of life in the company of others but also from our own addiction to noise, words, and activity.[26]
>
> Ruth Haley Barton

Solitude and silence are necessarily bound together. Dallas Willard's perspective is thought-provoking: "Just as silence is vital to make solitude real, so is solitude needed to make the discipline of silence complete."[27]

Exercising this discipline is rare today. In our culture we tend to turn on sound and surround ourselves with other people. I don't know how we ever expect to hear the voice of God.

Experiencing silence may feel uncomfortable if you aren't accustomed to it. If so, begin with short periods of time, maybe five minutes, extending it each day or each week. Settle into peace by sensing God's presence. Rid your mind of all distractions so that you are able to hear his voice. You might set aside a chair or area as a sacred space reserved for your meetings with God. Practice silence by turning off the television or radio while you do chores. Learn to relax without constant noise. I rarely turn on the television or radio when I am alone, and I have found that quiet is a friend to my soul.

Solitude and silence open our ears to hear God. When we encounter difficult people and trying circumstances, we need to discern what God is saying to us out of those experiences. Without focused time listening, we will not be transformed by the trials designed by God to build our character (James 1:2-4).

As a leader, you must learn to recognize the voice of God. If you have filled your life with sound, even if it's your own voice in prayer, you have no room to hear him speak. Seek to discern God's voice by silencing all others.

Sabbath Rest: Refraining from Work to Celebrate God

> Sabbath imparts the rest of God—actual physical, mental, spiritual rest, but also the *rest* of God—the things of God's nature and presence we miss in our busyness.[28]
>
> Mark Buchanan

Our culture is constantly on the move, but God designed us to have consistent periods of rest. When we fail to take time away from work, our spiritual, emotional, and physical health is jeopardized. God's best means that we incorporate rest into our regular routines.

At my best, I practice a weekly Sabbath. When I don't, I stress over work; I lose sleep; and I am not grateful or contented. When I choose to rest rather than work, I am forced to trust God to enable me to accomplish what is necessary in the remaining six days, stretching my faith.

How do we practice Sabbath without a legalistic list, such as the one created by the rabbis of old? What constitutes work? Buchanan gives us a guideline for determining what Sabbath looks like: "One thing is indispensable: to cease from that which is necessary. This is Sabbath's golden rule, the one rule to which all other rules distill. Stop doing what you ought to do. There are six days to do what you ought to do. Six days to be caught in the web of economic and political and social necessity. And then one day to take wing."[29] Sabbath was made to enjoy the things that are life-giving, unattached to our normal jobs. That means that what I do on Sabbath is different from what you do, so long as we avoid the "oughts."

Sabbath was made to enjoy the things that are life-giving, as Buchanan says, the things that give us wing!

Fasting: Refraining from God's Good Gifts to Focus on Him

> Fasting confirms our utter dependence upon God by finding in him a source of sustenance beyond food.[30]
>
> Dallas Willard

The purpose of biblical fasting is always spiritual. Hunger drives us to depend upon God and his power. Although it is not commanded in the New Testament, it is assumed (*i.e.*, Matthew 6:16-18; 9:15).

One yearly rhythm I practice is the celebration of Lent, during which I fast from a favorite food. I also fast periodically to focus on prayer for specific needs, but I recognize it is not a way to manipulate God.

If you have never fasted from food, you may be encouraged to learn that there are many ways to accomplish that. You may choose to take in water alone or drink juice as well. It is generally best for beginners to first undertake a short fast, perhaps daylight only, before moving on to longer ones. When I observe a day-long fast, I generally follow the Hebrew day from sundown to sundown. That means that I eat dinner early while the sun is still up. When I eat again the next evening after sundown, I have fasted for twenty-four hours. Going all night and the next day and night without food (thirty-six hours or so) is not healthy for me. I have more success this way, and it is very biblical. In order to grow in this discipline, begin with what works so that you enjoy success; only then, expand your fast.

Biblical fasting focuses on food and drink, but abstaining from other good gifts of God can also be beneficial. Consider pursuits that aren't necessarily bad activities but those that distract you from God. What about Facebook, chat rooms, television, talking on the phone, texting, time online, reading, surfing the web, or talk shows? Which of God's good gifts have a hold on you? You might think dessert, chocolate, movies, or books. What would be difficult to give up without depending on God's power and grace?

Christ calls his people to deny themselves (Matthew 16:24); fasting is a way we train in this godly quality. It draws us to depend upon God for the discipline and power to persevere through the fast.

Meditation: Extended Concentration and Focus on God and His Word

> Meditation is thinking seriously, carefully and reflectively on the truth of Scripture to the point of the Scripture integrating into all of your functioning life.[31]
>
> Dr. Gail Seidel

Meditation is an important biblical discipline. When God sent Joshua into the Promised Land as the new leader of the Hebrew nation, he said,

"This book of the law shall not depart from your mouth, but you shall meditate on it day and night, so that you may be careful to do according to all that is written in it; for then you will make your way prosperous, and then you will have success" (Josh. 1:8, NASB). Psalm 1 refers to those who meditate on God's Word day and night as blessed.

Don't confuse the practice of meditation in the Scriptures with that of the New Age movement. Richard Foster distinguishes the Christian practice from others: "It is this ethical call to repentance, to change, to obedience that most clearly distinguishes Christian meditation. . . . there is no loss of identity, no merging with cosmic consciousness, no fanciful astral travel. Rather, we are called to life-transforming obedience because we have encountered the God of Abraham, Isaac, and Jacob. Christ is truly present among us to heal us, to forgive us, to change us, to empower us."[32]

Biblically, meditation involves mulling over some scriptural truth or aspect of God's greatness and character. We may think about specific verses or consider the creation, focusing on the depths of what it reveals about God. The Psalms often overwhelm me with God's majesty as I slow down and allow truth to enter my soul. If the Scriptures have never left you stunned by who God is, stop and meditate upon the power and greatness of your God.

When I spend extended time outdoors, I consider the beauty and power of the Creator. I have found it immensely beneficial to combine solitude, silence, and a place to meditate into my schedule periodically.

Devotional Scripture Reading

> Devotional reading or hearing of Scripture requires an
> open, reflective, listening posture alert to the voice of God.
> This type of reading is aimed more at growing a relationship
> with God than gathering information about God.[33]
>
> Adele Ahlberg Calhoun

One method of devotional reading of God's word is *Lectio Divina* (divine reading), an ancient Christian spiritual practice which has enjoyed renewed interest in recent years. It involves oral reading of a section of Scripture and expectant listening for God's message.

Eugene Petersen encourages Christians to let God's Word speak to them through this kind of devotional reading in *Eat This Book* where he presents a helpful outline of *Lectio Divina*:

Lectio Divina comprises four elements: *lectio* (we read the text), *meditato* (we meditate the text), *oratio* (we pray the text) and *comtemplatio* (we live the text). . . There is a certain natural progression from one to another, but after separating them in order to understand them we find that in actual practice they are not four discrete items that we engage in one after another in stair-step fashion. Rather than linear the process is more like a looping spiral in which all four elements are repeated, but in various sequences and configurations. What we are after is noticing, seeing the interplay—elements not marching in precise formation but one calling forth another and then receding to give place to another, none in isolation from the others but thrown together in a kind of playful folk dance.[34]

When I find myself too engrossed in the meaning of the text, this spiritual discipline reminds me that God is speaking to me personally through his Word, asking me to live Scripture out in my own life. When my head is more involved than my heart, I appreciate the way this ancient practice draws me into the living voice of God.

Bible Study: Searching for the Meaning of Scripture

Bible study involves engaging the mind and focusing attention on Scripture in an attempt to understand and apply truth to every part of my life.[35]

Adele Ahlberg Calhoun

John 8:32 says that the truth sets us free. It is the Scripture that reveals who God is and what he has done. We cannot know him or his message to us apart from his Word. Its study must be a priority in the lives of those who want to be changed into the image of Jesus.

Study's purpose is to know and understand the truth. It is not devotional reading of the scriptures, which is purposed for application. It is impossible, however, to correctly apply without accurate interpretation, making Bible study foundational to application and devotion. I have been privileged to be trained through Precept Ministries[36] and Dallas Seminary in tools for studying the Bible inductively. If you don't know how to study on your own, please invest in a book or find a class that will give you the means to understand God's Word for yourself within its context. Every Christian who influences others must be a student of the Bible.

Jan Winebrenner says, "Study doesn't increase his love for us. It can, however, increase our love for him and enable us to travel this life with peace and wisdom."[37] We have to know who God really is in order to love him as we should; we have to hear from him in order to live as we should. Study of Scripture is essential to our spiritual lives.

Scripture Memorization

> Its desire: to carry the life-shaping words of God in me at all times and in all places[38]
>
> Adele Ahlberg Calhoun

The benefits of knowing God's Word are considerable. The Gospels reveal how often Jesus relied on Scripture, not only to resist temptation but also to challenge and refute those who opposed him. Psalm 119 abounds with specific benefits and blessings of God's Word. Verse 11 says, "I have hidden your word in my heart that I might not sin against you" (NIV).

When memorizing scripture, use a translation that communicates well to you. Verses that prompt you to walk in obedience or that touch a present situation will be easiest to remember. Learn passages that help you live out the life of Christ—those that speak truth where you tend to believe a lie or those that bolster your faith where it is weak.

I am grateful for vacation Bible school teachers who challenged me to memorize. I have lost the ability to remember as easily as I once did so I encourage you to learn as much scripture as you can now. What we do not review, we commonly lose. Find a way to organize your memory verses so that you consistently repeat them.

Just as Jesus constantly quoted scriptures that he knew by heart, we must have truth at our disposal when the situation requires it as well. As you study and read God's Word, continue memorizing those verses that impact your heart.

Simplicity

> Its desire: to uncomplicate and untangle my life so I can focus on what really matters[39]
>
> Adele Ahlberg Calhoun

STRENGTHENING YOUR CORE: CENTERED IN CHRIST

Simplicity begins with an inner focus on God which leads to a practical outward focus. It means prioritizing God's unseen kingdom over all else (Matthew 6:25-33), resulting in a simple lifestyle. True simplicity includes putting God first in all areas of life—with time, money, style of living, and activities.

In contrast to asceticism which renounces material possessions, simplicity delights in the many gifts of God's creation. Paul was content with both plenty and with little (Philippians 4:12). Although Jesus certainly led a life of simplicity, he also enjoyed feasts and celebrations such as the wedding in Cana and the dinner at Matthew's house (John 2:1-10; Luke 5:27-35), and he accepted the generosity of Mary of Bethany's anointing (John 12:1-8).

As I learn more about the world's poverty, I attempt to live more simply by distinguishing my needs from my desires, ridding my home of extras, and asking God to guide my time and spending. As a prosperous American, I find it very difficult to keep life simple, but I pray for wisdom in my attempts to grow in this area and invite you to join me in pursuit of simplicity.

Staying Centered

By practicing spiritual disciplines, we put ourselves in a position to intimately know God in an ongoing love relationship.

Kay Spinelli, who serves with her husband Terry as a missionary, graciously shares what she learned about the need for continued focus on Christ:

> As a new Christian, I was taught that in order to start growing I needed to develop the habit of practicing the basics of the Christian life – daily time in God's Word, prayer and Scripture memory. Even as I followed the instruction of those who taught me, I was convinced that someday I would discover a deeper secret of spiritual maturity that went far beyond the basics.
>
> I have now been a believer for thirty-nine years. Thirty-seven of them have been in vocational Christian ministry. Serving the Lord has taken me to many countries around the world and led me to adventures and challenges I never, never dreamed as a young Christian I would have.

The Lord has taught me much about staying centered on Christ and growing spiritually, but interestingly enough, at the core of those lessons lay the basics I learned as a new believer – time in God's Word, prayer, and Scripture memory.

I was reminded of this fact just a few months ago. My husband and I are presently living in India working with Indian Christians to spread the gospel in South Asia through establishing church planting movements. Recently, I found myself feeling distant from the Lord. Even though I was having regular prayer times and memorizing scripture, I had started excusing myself from a daily time in God's Word.

At that time, we hosted a retired, veteran missionary who had been on the mission field for thirty years. He came to India to do a conference for our ministry's national church planters. On the first day of the conference, he told us how Chinese believers encourage each other to grow spiritually by staying in God's Word. Every day they ask each other, "Have you eaten today?" The question has a dual meaning; it refers to both physical food and spiritual food. For example, if it is mid-morning and they ask, "Have you eaten today?" the expected answer is, "Yes, twice, once at breakfast and once in the Bible." The follow-up question is usually, "How did the Lord feed you?" The responder then shares what the Lord gave her that morning in her devotional. The missionary told us that the churches where the Chinese believers regularly asked and answered these questions saw great spiritual growth. Why? Because there was regular accountability and encouragement to be in and obey the Scriptures.

As our missionary friend spoke, I realized that I was feeling distant from the Lord because I had allowed myself to become complacent and lazy about spending daily time with Him in His Word. I also recognized that I needed to make myself more accountable to those around me in order to be encouraged to stay in and apply God's Word. It is way too easy for me to hide the fact that I'm not being consistent in my times with the Lord. It is truly possible to "talk the talk, but not walk the walk." I have to choose to allow other Christians to be involved in that part of my relationship with God so I ask my husband and two of my Indian friends to ask me "Have you eaten today?" on a regular basis.

The truth about the "basics" of the Christian life is that they are really the "essentials" of the Christian life. We each need to do whatever it takes to build the habit of spending time with the Lord and maintaining it.[40]

I appreciate Kay's wisdom and transparency. Spiritual disciplines are not only necessary for growth as a new believer, but they are essential for Christians of every age and level of maturity to stay vitally connected to Christ. The need for accountability that she discovered is essential to keep a spiritual core strong. That is why the Personal Action Plan associated with each fundamental requires finding support in Christ's body.

Although physical training is hard for me, I subject myself to it, knowing it is for my best. Hopefully, I will discipline my life beyond the physical to include spiritual exercises that draw me closer to the heart of God. Why don't you join the adventure of intimacy with Christ?

Personal Action Plan

Chapter 2: Strengthening your Core

Assessment

Read Psalm 63. What words/phrases reveal the depth of David's relationship with God?

Sit quietly before God, asking him for insight as to how centered your life is in Christ and then answer the following questions:

Rate how consistently you spend time with God on a scale of 1-10, with 1 meaning totally inconsistent and 10 being always consistent, never missing.

Circle all the words/phrases below that best describe your usual time with God:

Hurried	Obligatory	Meaningful	Distracted
Worshipful	Thankful	Self-focused	Peace-giving
Full of awe	Prayer lists	Spirit-led	God-focused
My agenda	God's agenda	Meditative	Timed
Relaxed	Joyful	Short	Emotionally real
My answers	God's answers		

In light of your answers on the first two questions, how would you rate your quality of time with God on scale of 1-10, with 1 being rote and 10 being intimate and real? Why?

During your average time with God, what percentage of your time is spent—

_____ In awe and worship of him?
_____ Reading or meditating on his Word?

_____ Focused on your prayer requests?
_____ Listening in silence and stillness?

Ask God what your previous answers reveal about your love relationship with him. How centered are you on God himself—hearing him, knowing him, worshipping him? Write down your insights.

Challenge
What is your plan to grow more centered on God? What needs to change in your attitude and your practice?

What will you do differently this week to challenge yourself? What will you change from your usual practice? What new spiritual discipline will you try?

Support
What kind of support do you need on a consistent basis in order to grow in this area? Consider these ideas and come up with a workable plan of your own.

+ A prayer/accountability partner. (If so, whom will you approach?)
+ Sharing this as a prayer request with a community to which you are already attached and continuing to update them as to how you are doing.
+ Keeping a daily log of your quiet time and reviewing it each week with another person. Will you agree to be accountable to what the person says? If so, who will it be?

Your plan for support:

Summary of my Plan:
My challenge(s):

My support in reaching this challenge:

Chapter 3

Dirty Laundry
Character

> Leadership development is a lifelong journey in which our sovereign God orchestrates the experiences, crises, and tests of life to develop in a man or woman those qualities essential to godly leadership. Beyond developing leadership skills, it is more the progressive development of those inner qualities that enables a skilled person to be a godly servant leader. Who you *are* as a leader determines what you do in leading. [41]
>
> Andrew Seidel

When I was a little girl, we didn't have a clothes dryer. (I do realize this dates me, but we did have a washer, if that helps.) It was necessary to hang our clean clothing outside on the backyard clothesline to dry. In the southern Texas climate, it didn't take more than a few hours for the sun to produce the heat necessary for the drying process. (Now I appreciate how green and energy efficient this method was. Today our neighborhood homeowner's association would likely fine us if we put out a clothesline.) There were times, however, when rain interrupted the sun's work. I have vivid memories of my mother yelling at my sister and me to run outside and help her get the clothes in quickly before they got wetter than they already were. After the showers were over, we ran back out and hung them up again.

Because everyone had clotheslines and there were few fences to obstruct the view, the proverbial saying not to air your dirty laundry was clear. Just as we would never put dirty clothes on the line for everyone in the neighborhood to see, we considered it rude and embarrassing to talk about family problems and failings in public. In fact, my mother frowned upon mentioning anything negative about a family member unless, of course, we were gossiping with someone else in the family. But with others we pretended to be upstanding and even perfect people, no matter how far away from reality that was.

We had an uncle who was a bootlegger during Prohibition, but my sister and I had instructions not to discuss that with anyone. And we certainly didn't mention the divorces that aunts and cousins had experienced. I was grown before anyone told me that another uncle was an alcoholic; I only learned about it then because of his renewed drinking. Even a mild difference of opinion within the family was not part of our conversations. I learned to hide who I really was.

This thinking permeated not only our culture but that of the church as well. I never remember anyone confessing anything. Church was the place for saints, not real sinners. Only people who committed sins prevalent in the congregation were allowed. (Each denomination seemed to have its own pet sins.) On Sundays we dressed up to look good. Our perfect appearances represented what we wanted others to believe about our lives.

Although things have changed a lot in the American church, there is a continued reluctance for many believers to air their dirty laundry. Despite the many wonderful opportunities to receive help from support groups, twelve-step recovery programs, prayer, counseling, and marriage programs, we are often afraid to reveal who we really are, expecting judgment and gossip rather than grace. Although criticism and ostracism still occur in some churches (and I hate it), it is impossible to reach our potential as leaders if we refuse to face the reality of who we really are before God and others.

The Light Reveals our Dirt

As we become more centered on Christ (remember our first leadership essential in chapter 2), we begin to see the truth about ourselves as his light shines into our souls. The more clearly we view Jesus, the more we recognize where we fall short of his grace, love, and perfection. We either choose to deal with what we see or move away from the light and avoid the dirt within.

Our second essential of leadership is character, but what is that? Consider these insights:

+ Dwight L. Moody suggests that it is "what you are in the dark."[42]
+ Oswald Chambers describes it this way: "Character in a saint means the disposition of Jesus Christ persistently manifested."[43]
+ Thomas Paine recognizes it is not always consistent with what others believe about us: "Reputation is what men and women think of us. Character is what God and the angels know of us."[44]

As women who desire to influence others, we must grow in character, always moving closer to the light and asking God for the grace to change. We know that he hears us and forgives us as we confess our sins; we also recognize that he gives us the power to change by his Spirit. It all starts with airing our dirty laundry before him in heart-felt confession.

"But if we confess our sins, he is faithful and righteous, forgiving us our sins and cleansing us from all unrighteousness" (1 John 1:9).

It is important to not only know intellectually that we are forgiven by Jesus's death on the cross, but we must also experience it by trusting his daily forgiveness. A healthy leader does not live in guilt and shame because she knows God's grace and love. It is impossible to grow more like Jesus if we are bound up in the belief that we must live up to certain expectations before God loves and accepts us. He desires us to follow him and his commands, not in order to gain his approval but so that we live in ways that are best for us and those around us. God's hope is that we choose abundant lives—full of love, obedience, and grace.

The reality, however, is that we all fall short of aligning our lives with God's best. We continue to sin while we live in bodies of flesh. None of us is perfect, whether we are pastors, moms, or counselors. So what do we do when God reveals our dirt?

Our first choice is to uncover our sins before God and also at times with those whom we want to influence. The Bible instructs us to admit our sins to fellow believers: "So confess your sins to one another and pray for one another so that you may be healed" (James 5:16). As we open ourselves to one another, we unlock opportunities for support, accountability, and wisdom from the community of faith. Being honest about who we really are frees us from the tyranny of image and perfectionism. (Of course, we must carefully choose what to share and with whom. Wisdom and discretion are important qualities to prevent us from saying too much. When I am uncertain about the audience or the specifics, I limit my confessions to generalities.)

Teresa of Avila suggests this guideline: "Be gentle to all and stern with yourself."[45] Instead, we tend to do just the opposite—criticize others and go easy on ourselves.

I hate admitting that it is comfortable for me to find faults in others and feel the pride of my self-righteousness. Instead of comparing myself to those around me, I ought to look closely into God's Word to see myself in truth and deal with my dirt. Regularly I try to sit silently before God and allow him to reveal anything I have missed about myself. It's not always pretty or comfortable to take a hard look into my own heart, but it brings the freedom of forgiveness and the possibility of repairing relationships with others that have been affected by my sins.

The second option for dealing with our sins is to hide the truth from others although we confess it to God. That scenario limits our connection with those we lead. It fosters the suggestion that we are perfect, or close to it. Christians who cloak their issues become hypocrites because they wear masks designed to fool others. We must be willing to honestly confront our own sins and be vulnerable enough to share what we discover about ourselves with those we influence. I find this very tough to do, especially after years of being taught that it is improper to discuss such things. I have apologized to individuals and even groups of people when God convicted me of a sin, especially when it affected my relationships with them. As I teach, I often share some sins and shortcomings that God's Word has brought to light as they apply to the lesson.

The final alternative is to refuse to take responsibility for our sins at all. When we fail to recognize and confess them, we likely only fool ourselves. Others often see what we deny, and our leadership may be compromised.

God Is Doing the Dirty Work

God is at work to transform his children so that we look like Jesus. The theological term for this process is sanctification, which means "set apart" in Greek. We are positionally sanctified when we trust Jesus, being set aside as God's own possession—a wonderful truth. There is a second practical aspect of sanctification, however, that makes us progressively more like the Savior. We are set more and more apart from the people we used to be as we live out our new lives. Dallas Willard says that Jesus came to bring "a revolution of character, which proceeds by changing people from the inside through ongoing personal relationship to God in Christ and to one another."[46]

What means does God use as he remolds us into the character of Jesus?

Galatians 5:22, 23 gives this insight into one method that God uses for change: "But the fruit of the Spirit is love, joy, peace, patience, kindness, goodness, faithfulness, gentleness, and self-control. Against such things there is no law."

God's Spirit lives within all believers in Christ, producing fruit that includes this list of qualities. The more we depend on God day by day, the more he reveals himself through our character. As we considered our previous fundamental, centered in Christ, we saw that we produce fruit only when we are connected to the Vine, Jesus. As we focus on our relationship with him, we see changes in our attitudes and actions as he transforms our hearts. The lack of such traits indicates that we are living apart from the power and control of God's Spirit.

Just this week I was reminded of my tendency to get so engrossed in my tasks that I fail to be kind and patient. In this case my short, blunt e-mail hurt a sweet woman who wasn't really sure how to take it. Although I apologized and our relationship is better, I am reminded once again of my sinfulness and lack of care when I put my focus on things rather than people. I see this weakness, but too often I forget to depend upon God's Spirit to do something different in me, even in the small things—like e-mails.

Another method of growth that God uses is circumstances. As Paul explains, God purposes situations and experiences to mold our hearts: "And we know that all things work together for good for those who love God, who are called according to his purpose, because those whom he foreknew he also predestined to be conformed to the image of his Son, that his Son would be the firstborn among many brothers and sisters" (Romans 8:28-29).

James mentions a specific type of situation that God uses to change our character:

> My brothers and sisters, consider it nothing but joy when you fall into all sorts of trials, because you know that the testing of your faith produces endurance. And let endurance have its perfect effect, so that you will be perfect and complete, not deficient in anything. . . . Happy is the one who endures testing, because when he has proven to be genuine, he will receive the crown of life that God promised to those who love him (James 1:2-4, 12).

Even in hard times, God builds character, resulting in our perfection and completion. That sounds a bit optimistic to me, but it makes more sense when I realize that the Greek meanings for perfection and completion suggest maturity and wholeness, not lacking any part. God takes hard times to prepare us for a life of faith.

The key is to look for God's message as we encounter difficulties with people or with situations. Asking God what he desires to teach us opens our hearts to respond to his voice. When life is hard, we have an opportunity to discover specific areas of needed change. Our natural tendency is to blame others in anger and bitterness, but God wants us to shine his light in our souls so that we deal with our own issues. That is what happened to Jennifer Radabaugh:

> A few years ago my husband and I knew that God was calling us to minister at a church here in the Dallas area. It was not an easy thing to do because it meant leaving our very comfortable life. Both of our families lived within ten minutes of us. We had many dear neighbors and close friends. Most weekends we cooked out with our neighbors while everyone's kids played for hours up and down the street. It meant saying goodbye to a church we had served at for over ten years. But we knew that we would miss out on what God wanted to do in us and through us if we didn't follow his leading.

> We called it God's great adventure and looked forward to what lay ahead. We grew closer as a family and closer to the Lord because we were all we had. The Lord showed us his goodness every day in little and big ways. He answered so many prayers of concern we had for our children in their transition. Yes, there were tears when we missed our friends and felt lonely but it didn't take long before we plugged into our church, neighborhood and schools. God continued to take me out of my comfort zone as I was asked to lead a small group women's Bible study. I began to develop some deeper relationships with women and staff wives and was so blessed by their faith and friendship. For two years, we had the privilege of hosting a community group in our home once a week and truly enjoyed doing life together. They became our family away from family and Dallas now felt like home.

But this is not where the story ends. Much to my surprise God had other plans. One day I found my husband at home around 10:00 on a Monday morning. He began to share with me that several staff had been laid off due to budget shortfalls and he was one of them. We were both in shock. I felt like a balloon that had been punctured and I was deflating. What was going on? This was not the plan or at least not mine. When you lose a job it's hard enough but when your job is your church, you lose a family as well.

Moments later, I realized that God had actually prepared me earlier that morning for this very news. I grabbed my devotion book and showed it to my husband. It read: "Trust Me by relinquishing control into My hands. Let go, and recognize that I am God. . . When you bring me prayer requests, lay out your concerns before Me. Then thank Me for the answers that I have set in motion long before you can discern the results. Keep your focus on My presence and My promises. . ."[47]

I knew then that God was in the midst of doing something. I didn't have to like it, but it was out of my control, and all either of us could do was to trust him. The next few weeks I poured out my heart to him and spent hours in his Word. The more time I spent, the more he showed me things about myself that I needed to surrender to him. For example, letting go of the hurt and anger I felt over the situation. Through his Word, God was transforming me by renewing my mind and changing the way I viewed my current circumstances. I found that in God's presence there was peace. I can't truly explain it, but somehow I wasn't worried about our future. My prayers changed from, "Father, show us what you have next," to "Father, help me not to miss what you want to teach me." I am truly grateful that God was more concerned about my character than my comfort. And that he wanted to do a work in me so that I could become more effective in reaching the world for Christ.[48]

God used Jennifer's trial to teach her to view circumstances through faith rather than through anger and hurt. As a result, she grew as a woman of character.

God not only uses our situations, especially the difficulties, but he also uses other means to change our hearts. Again, James comments:

> But be sure you live out the message and do not merely listen to it and so deceive yourselves. For if someone merely listens to the message and does not live it out, he is like someone who gazes at his own face in a mirror. For he gazes at himself and then goes out and immediately forgets what sort of person he was. But the one who peers into the perfect law of liberty and fixes his attention there, and does not become a forgetful listener but one who lives it out – he will be blessed in what he does (James 1:22-25).

God employs his Word to transform us when we listen and apply the truth found there.

Early in my marriage I experienced a lot of frustration with my husband. As I began to grow in my faith, I prayed for him, asking God to change him in the areas where I wanted him to be different, but God didn't seem to be quite as concerned as I was about the improvements that I was suggesting. Instead, he sent someone who recommended a book, *Lord, Change Me!* by Evelyn Christenson.[49] The author proposed that the issues may be my fault and not entirely problems that my husband needed to fix. Instead of looking for the speck in his eye, I needed to be more concerned about the log in my own (Matthew 7:3). Although I was looking in the mirror of God's Word, I was too busy noticing someone else's dirt to wash off my own.

God convicted me to focus on myself rather than my husband as I read the Scripture. Rather than telling God how to change him into my idea of the perfect man, I began to pray that I would become a better wife. You are likely not surprised to learn that our marriage improved a great deal once I allowed God to use his Word to speak to me about my character. I am not sure that my husband changed at all.

The Bible gives us insight into ourselves, calling us to respond to the dirt we see there. But if we refuse to listen, God purposes to change us, even when we don't like it.

And have you forgotten the exhortation addressed to you as sons? "My son, do not scorn the Lord's discipline or give up when he corrects you. For the Lord disciplines the one he loves and chastises every son he accepts." Endure your suffering as discipline; God is treating you as sons. For what son is there that a father does not discipline? But if you do not experience discipline, something all sons have shared in, then you are illegitimate and are not sons. Besides, we have experienced discipline from our earthly fathers and we respected them; shall we not submit ourselves all the more to the Father of spirits and receive life? For they disciplined us for a little while as seemed good to them, but he does so for our benefit, that we may share his holiness. Now all discipline seems painful at the time, not joyful. But later it produces the fruit of peace and righteousness for those trained by it. Therefore, strengthen your listless hands and your weak knees, and make straight paths for your feet, so that what is lame may not be put out of joint but be healed (Hebrews 12:5-13).

It is impossible for us to identify when God is disciplining another person for her sins. Some misguided Christian leaders have suggested that only those who have sinned will ever have problems because God doesn't ever bring hurt or need into our lives. That is not a scriptural teaching, as all the passages we just considered clearly reveal. God is at work to get rid of the dirt in our lives and make us like Jesus. He uses all sorts of methods, and one of those is trials. Sometimes he disciplines us because we refuse to listen any other way, but hard times aren't necessarily the result of a refusal to repent. In either case when we face difficulties, we can know that God has a purpose to use the situation for our good and his glory. He will see us through it and give us the grace and power to persevere if we turn to him. By it, he will grow our character.

Training in Godliness

Because character is essential to Christian influence, God is in the business of producing it in us. However, we also carry responsibility. There is often a biblical tension between God's work and our responsibility to act. Although

God receives the credit because he is the one changing us, we are accountable to put ourselves in a place where he can work.

Spiritual disciplines, such as those we considered in the previous chapter, furnish a way of providing time and space to hear from God about his message and its application to our lives. They open our hearts to discern his gentle voice of conviction. Yes, they help us to grow in our love relationship with our Heavenly Father, but they are also one of his means of changing us.

Self-discipline is essential in fulfilling our responsibility to grow in character: "Train yourself for godliness. For 'physical exercise has some value, but godliness is valuable in every way. It holds promise for the present life and for the life to come.' This saying is trustworthy and deserves full acceptance. In fact this is why we work hard and struggle, because we have set our hope on the living God, who is the Savior of all people, especially of believers" (1 Timothy 4:7-10).

Becoming women who look like Jesus requires work and time. We practice spiritual disciplines and spend time with God, and he uses those opportunities to transform us into the image of Jesus. Character comes from the heart and works out in our lives through our external actions.

God's Word is foundational in our training. "For the word of God is living and active and sharper than any double-edged sword, piercing even to the point of dividing soul from spirit, and joints from marrow; it is able to judge the desires and thoughts of the heart" (Hebrews 4:12). As we place ourselves in a position to hear from God by spending time in the Scripture, he is able to reveal what is in our hearts. If we open ourselves to the truth of his message, he often points out various idols residing in his place—self being the primary one. In order for God to be God in our lives and for us to have the character of Jesus, it is necessary to tear them down and give God his rightful position.

It can also be beneficial to practice spiritual disciplines that counter specific sinful tendencies. The discipline of giving can help us learn to be gracious and generous instead of greedy. The idol of self requires us to serve ourselves rather than others; dethroning self may include finding ways to serve others secretly in menial ways. (Both giving and serving are considered spiritual disciplines, especially for those of us who don't have these spiritual gifts.) The Personal Action Plan will help you find methods that fit your particular weaknesses.

As you train for godliness, remember that only God can change you from the inside out. Willard puts it this way: "Though we must act, the resources for spiritual formation extend far beyond the human. They come from the interactive presence of the Holy Spirit in the lives of those who place their confidence in Christ."[50]

The Dirt was Flying

As I look back on my life, I can see changes; God has been maturing me through situations and his Word. He has put people and circumstances in my path to build my character. Those who know me recognize how far I still need to go, but those who have known me long enough also see how far I have come by God's grace.

One of my most difficult trials caused some of my character issues to surface that were preventing me from being the godly leader I needed to be. Many years ago, a couple in our church slandered me, accusing me of things I had never even thought, much less acted upon. They judged my motives, which they couldn't possibly know; they suggested that I was out for my own glory and wasn't fit to be in leadership. They said all of this to the other leaders involved in their particular ministry, and then they lambasted me over the phone. There was nothing kind, loving, or redeeming about their attitude or their words. They weren't trying to help me grow but wanted to keep me away from their territory in the church and said so. Most of their information was secondhand gossip and the rest was supposition. The little truth in it was based on events that were at least eight years old.

Months before their phone call, they attempted to influence me against another Bible teacher in the church. Instead of jumping on their side, I sought guidance from the pastoral staff by handing over the letter the couple had given me and then writing them a reply. This may have been their payback, but God purposed this attack for my good, not my destruction. Although their charges were unfair, listening to them caused me to run to God with the situation. I sat in solitude and silence with him for long periods of time, seeking answers. I asked him for insight into their accusations—what was true and what wasn't? Although their slanderous words were untrue, the situation did reveal major character issues inside of me. God helped me recognize that I often had a critical attitude similar to theirs. I was appalled to realize that I had likely misjudged other people based on gossip or actions long past, just as they had me. Grace and love were sometimes absent in my heart, and I looked more like the couple who slandered me than Jesus.

God used the unfair attack to make me more gracious, less judgmental, and less prone to believe stories about others. As a leader these lessons have served me well. Just this past year, a woman who worked with me in ministry for a number of years e-mailed me saying that I was the one person who accepted her without judging her. If true, it is only because God took a very hard time and used it to make me more like Jesus. I am grateful that he continues to work in my life to complete his work in me (Philippians 1:6).

Leaders aren't perfect but should be moving toward godliness. Those who walk with us as we lead should be able to trust our integrity and our hearts. They should know that our motives are pure and our word is true. We should be so honest about our sins and failures that we are the same people on the outside and the inside.

A Leader Like Jesus

Leaders reveal their character in the way they direct others. Jesus taught his disciples about the kind of leadership expected of his followers:

> You know that the rulers of the Gentiles lord it over them, and those in high positions use their authority over them. It must not be this way among you! Instead whoever wants to be great among you must be your servant, and whoever wants to be first among you must be your slave—just as the Son of Man did not come to be served but to serve, and to give his life as a ransom for many (Matthew 20:25-28).

Jesus modeled servant-leadership by coming to earth to give his life up for us. Paul provides specifics in Philippians 2:5-11:

> You should have the same attitude toward one another that Christ Jesus had, who though he existed in the form of God did not regard equality with God as something to be grasped, but emptied himself by taking on the form of a slave, by looking like other men, and by sharing in human nature. He humbled himself, by becoming obedient to the point of death– even death on a cross! As a result God exalted him and gave him the name that is above every name, so that at the name of Jesus every knee will bow– in heaven and on earth and under the earth – and every tongue confess that Jesus Christ is Lord to the glory of God the Father.

These passages identify a servant-leader as one who sacrifices for the sake of others, willingly gives up position and rights, and obeys God's will.

Jesus was the ultimate servant-leader, and he asked his disciples to mimic him. On the night he was betrayed, he illustrated this teaching by washing their feet. John records the story:

> So when Jesus had washed their feet and put his outer clothing back on, he took his place at the table again and said to them, "Do you understand what I have done for you? You call me 'Teacher' and 'Lord,' and do so correctly, for that is what I am. If I then, your Lord and Teacher, have washed your feet, you too ought to wash one another's feet. For I have given you an example– you should do just as I have done for you. I tell you the solemn truth, the slave is not greater than his master, nor is the one who is sent as a messenger greater than the one who sent him. If you understand these things, you will be blessed if you do them" (John 13:12-17).

Calvin Miller, in his book *The Empowered Leader*, says that the servant-leader runs on two tracks, like a train: the first track is total dependence upon the Savior and devotion to him, and the second track is the pursuit of God's agenda, not her own. Such leaders are not in it for themselves, their own glory, or their own significance. They are motivated solely by the glory of God.[51]

What does servant-leadership look like in a practical sense? Ted Engstrom tells this story:

> A friend of mine once visited a friend of his in a little church in Connecticut. He had been there for many years, preaching to a handful of people. My friend said to him one day, when he saw the minister washing the church windows, "What in the world are you doing?" He was occupied with every menial task in the church--many tasks that could have been turned over to high-school students or men and women in the church. His answer appeared pious and commendable--actually it was tragic. He said, "I do everything myself (to demonstrate his self-sacrificing). I run off my own bulletins. I wash the windows in the

church, as you can see. I put out the hymnbooks. I do everything... This way I know it's done properly." Was that a minister in the best sense?[52]

Is that true servant-leadership? No, it's not the significance of the task that determines whether someone is a servant. Doing menial work isn't the crux of biblical leadership. When I look for new leaders, I note selflessness, the willingness to give up personal time and energy for others, love for those they serve, and evidence of seeking God's glory over personal success.

Iorg says, "Servant leadership is, in its essence, an attitude. Servant leadership is defined more by who you are than by what you do."[53]

It's interesting how little importance God gives to skills and how much he gives to character. That is one reason that I usually look for new leaders from within my ministry. I rely on others who can personally recommend someone. When a woman unknown to the group seeks a leadership role, I ask her to participate in our community for a length of time before we use her in that capacity. An unwillingness to sit back and watch and learn may reveal self-promotion rather than service. A servant's spirit submits to the requests of those in leadership and willingly awaits God's timing.

A final passage is essential to assessing ourselves as servant-leaders:

> If I speak in the tongues of men and of angels, but I do not have love, I am a noisy gong or a clanging cymbal. And if I have prophecy, and know all mysteries and all knowledge, and if I have all faith so that I can remove mountains, but do not have love, I am nothing. If I give away everything I own, and if I give over my body in order to boast, but do not have love, I receive no benefit. And now these three remain: faith, hope, and love. But the greatest of these is love (1 Corinthians 13:1-3, 13).

If we are motivated by anything other than love of God and love for others, we shouldn't be influencing anyone. Although each of us will have days when we are merely doing what we have to do out of duty, love is what inspires a true servant-leader.

As Christian leaders, our character does count; in fact, it counts most. Whether you are influencing your children, mentoring a co-worker, or steering a team planning an event, your integrity will be the determining factor in how well you shape their future. If you center your life in Christ and that relationship, open yourself up to God's prompting about sins and idols in your life, train yourself in godliness, and air your dirty laundry so that who you are is consistent in public and private, you give God opportunities to develop your character and enhance your impact on others.

Personal Action Plan

Chapter 3: Dirty Laundry

Assessment

These scriptures mention qualities that God's leaders should exhibit. Sit quietly before God, asking him for insight as you assess your character in light of these verses, led by the questions.

Write down qualities God values according to the following passages: Proverbs 31:10-31; Ephesians 5:22-24, 33; 1 Timothy 2:9-11; 5:3-6, 9-13; Titus 2:3-5; 1 Peter 3:1-6. (Consider the character of the wife revealed by her action, not the activities themselves which may be determined by her culture.)

These verses are not specifically for women, but they outline qualities important for leaders. Write down any virtues not already on your list: Ephesians 4:1-3, 31-32; 1 Timothy 3:1-10; 2 Timothy 2:2; Titus 1:1-9; 1 Peter 5:1-9.

Review the qualities from this book chapter and list them below.

Go back to your lists and prayerfully rate yourself on each quality. Choose one of these ratings: S (strength), W (weakness), I (inconsistency).

Now consider what God may be showing you about yourself as you struggle through a present trial or hardship. Consider your attitude (such things as forgiveness, bitterness, envy, and anger), the strength of the faith that you have evidenced through it, and the fruit of the Spirit (Galatians 5:22-23). Then, write down areas of character weakness.

How would you rate yourself overall in character on a 1-10 scale with 10 being the character of Jesus? Why did you choose that number?

Review what you read about servant-leadership in the section "Jesus' Kind of Leader." Consider the factors below and how they affect your motivation and write down what God shows you about your heart:

- Love for those who follow you
- Devotion to God
- Desire to pursue God's agenda rather than your own
- Seeking God's glory over personal attention
- Willingness to sacrifice for those who follow you

Spend time confessing the sins that God has uncovered. Recognize that he forgives completely but he does want us to repent and not keep repeating the same failures. He will give us the grace and power to succeed when we are serious about growing in character to become more like Jesus.

Challenge

Think through the possibility that you need to confess to others. What confessions do you need to make to those whom you have offended or hurt? Are you hiding who you really are? Are you trying to be someone you are not? Are you enslaved by your image? Write down to whom you need to confess and what you need to tell them.

How do these scriptures challenge you as you think about what God has shown you about your character: Philippians 2:12; 1 Timothy 4:7; 6:11; 2 Peter 1:5-7?

Spiritual disciplines can help us open ourselves to God's work concerning areas of weakness or idolatry in our lives. Consider an area where you struggle. Is there a corresponding spiritual discipline (an opposite perhaps) that can be a way of personal training in overcoming it? Examples: 1. Secret giving if you seek attention or reward for what you do for others; 2. Fasting if you lack discipline; 3. Simplicity when your idol is materialism; 4. Sabbath-keeping if your idol is work or success.

You get the idea. In solitude and silence let God guide you. Write down what he shows you.

With what one character quality is God impressing you? What will you do about it? For example, if you need to become more hospitable, whom will you invite to your home and host? If you need to become more faithful, what have you said you would do and not followed through? Maybe you should write a note of apology to the person you let down. If you need to be more industrious, how will you keep yourself from wasting time and use it wisely instead? (If you can't think of what to do, contact your prayer partner from previous weeks or a mature believer and brainstorm ideas.) Perhaps spending more time with God and letting his Spirit fill you is the best thing you can do. Write down your plan.

Support

Share your plan with your prayer partner or another mature Christian by phone or email. Pray for one another on the phone if possible.

Summary of my Plan:

My challenge(s):

My support in reaching this challenge:

Chapter 4

Take the Wind with You
Calling Part 1

> The truth is not that God is finding us a place for our gifts but that God has created us and our gifts for a place of his choosing—and we will only be ourselves when we are finally there.[54]
>
> Os Guinness

The third essential of leadership is calling, which is God's overarching purpose for a particular person. Think of it as the big picture of what God has called you to uniquely contribute with the life he has given you. You might visualize it as a broad umbrella that covers your entire lifetime, both career and personal. I will also use the word mission for this concept, but it's not a "c" word like the other essentials. However, you may prefer to think of it as your mission, God's specific life purpose for you.

When I use the term calling as a leadership essential, I am not referring to those things to which God calls all Christians; we are summoned to be God's people, to love him, and to bring him glory. All believers are to pursue these things; there is nothing unique about them. The mission I am discussing is distinctive to you, giving you a specific function in God's kingdom.

Calling builds on the previous two essentials, centered in Christ and character. Both of these involve the overarching command to love God with all our hearts, souls, minds, and strength. We do not pursue our particular calling; instead, we pursue Jesus. As that relationship works out in practical living, he uses us to complete the work that he has designed for us. We don't have to look for it; he brings it to us as an outgrowth of what is inside—our

49

love relationship with him. If he isn't our primary concern, we don't need to be influencing or leading others.

Guinness verbalizes this idea: "We are not primarily called to do something or go somewhere; we are called to Someone. We are not called first to special work but to God. The key to answering the call is to be devoted to no one and to nothing above God Himself."[55]

Richard Nelson Bolles puts it this way: "Your first mission on earth is one you share with the rest of the human race, but it is no less your individual Mission for the fact that it is shared: and that is, to seek to stand hour by hour in the conscious presence of God, the One from whom your mission is derived. The Missioner before the Mission is the rule."[56]

Once God himself is your first priority, you are ready to discover your personal mission.

Now, don't think in terms of short-term activities or goals. For example, consider the differences involved in going on a two-week mission trip and becoming a lifetime missionary. I have been on four short-term mission trips, and I have never really changed my life because of them. There were some adjustments for a few weeks but nothing long lasting. On the other hand, career missionaries' assignments are far reaching and take place over many years. Because their focus in life becomes the mission, they adjust everything to it. They may move from one location to the next or one ministry to another, but the course of their lives is set by their calling. In the same way, your mission covers your lifetime and incorporates every aspect of your life.

God chooses us individually and specifically to fulfill plans that he has for us; he prepares us by gifting us and maturing us to do the exact work that he has called us to do. "For by grace you are saved through faith, and this is not from yourselves, it is the gift of God; it is not from works, so that no one can boast. For we are his workmanship, having been created in Christ Jesus for good works that God prepared beforehand so we may do them" (Ephesians 2:8-10).

You and I were in the mind and plans of God long before we ever knew him. He had specific goals for each of us, the good works for which he prepared us by developing and gifting us. How great is it that God would allow us to be part of his work on earth! We are Plan A for building his kingdom, and each of us has a specific role in that plan.

Recently *O: The Oprah Magazine* featured "What's Your True Calling? An Easy-Does-It Guide to Finding and Fulfilling Your Life's Purpose."[57] Calling is such a basic concept to life that even the secular world notices that it affects a person's work satisfaction. Just as I am encouraging you to discover and develop in the area of your calling, this series of articles also suggests people focus on their abilities and passions. However, they miss the essential—that the God who created us has given each of us a unique calling, not to fulfill ourselves but to realize his kingdom purposes in our lives.

Don't Confuse your Calling!

So often I find people confused about their calling, which leads to uncertainty in life direction.

Not a Job

Your mission isn't your job. For ten years I worked on church staffs leading women's ministries, but that is not my calling. God's plan for me is more than these jobs; they are not the totality of what God has asked me to do in a unique way with my life. I was fulfilling my mission for many years before I got those positions, and now that I am no longer on a church staff, I continue to realize my calling. The job was merely one way of obeying God's invitation to serve him in specific ways.

Vickie Kraft was a pioneer in women's ministries in the U.S. and one of my predecessors at Northwest Bible Church. The mission that God laid on her heart many years ago was to mentor women through the teaching of God's Word. Although she has been retired from the position for over twelve years now, she continues to invest in the lives of younger women through small group Bible studies in her home. Now the women come to her as she continues to fulfill the good works that God prepared for her life. Her mission is ongoing because it is bigger than a job.

Not a Role, like Wife or Mother or Professional

The various roles that we fill throughout our lives are certainly connected to the general call to love, obey, and glorify God, and through them, we may help satisfy our personal missions as well. However, such functions are not synonymous with calling because they may not continue for a lifetime. Statistics reveal that most women will outlive their husbands, and many others will divorce. Our children will all grow up and leave us behind. Our professional lives can end quickly with health issues or economic downturns. Instead of equating to our individual missions, our roles are simply one arena through which we live them out.

My children are now grown and gone. If I had seen myself only in terms of being a mother, I would now be lost because I have done my job and moved into a different phase in my relationship with them. Sadly, I have friends who placed all of their time and energy into parenting, seeing it as their only calling. As their children have left and developed independent lives, these women feel purposeless and lost, and many deal with depression. Often, they seek to fill the void by controlling and meddling in their children's lives with sad results.

When you think of calling, think bigger and more long term than any role.

Not Necessarily Grand or Highly Visible

Every believer has a personal calling, not just pastors or missionaries—or Beth Moore. Each of us is summoned to particular good works, as we saw in Ephesians. You may be called to love and care for the hurting and the outcast in practical ways, which will never involve a highly visible role. Few may ever notice that you are busy on God's mission, but you bring the love of God to both believers and unbelievers and produce God's kingdom on earth in tangible ways.

I have been privileged to co-labor with women who served behind the scenes in the Bible studies which I have taught; I think of women like Twylla. Although she was not as visible as I was, her contributions were just as important. She was the hands of Christ extended with warmth and welcome to others by organizing and serving snacks and drinks. Evelyn is another such leader. Without her we would not have succeeded with our audio-visual equipment many, many times. Her labor to record my talks and format them for bible.org has allowed women all over the world to benefit. Evelyn's mission involves serving others with the love of Jesus by using her skills to support and extend the ministries of other believers.

Not Vision

Although calling isn't the same as vision, we do need vision to accomplish it. (I am defining vision as a particular picture of the future. We will look at vision in a later chapter.) We can see the difference in Noah's life. As he built the ark, he followed his calling to be God's witness to his world by warning his neighbors of coming judgment (2 Peter 2:5). There was little fruit from his preaching; none of his neighbors came to repentance. Only his sons and their wives responded and were saved from drowning. That doesn't diminish the call on Noah's life because mission is not about results. Noah's vision, on the other hand, was to build an ark to save lives in a flood, and he did accomplish that God-given goal.

Patricia's Story

When I met Patricia, she was confused about her calling. When a number of women in her MOPS[58] group wanted her to continue with them another year, she wondered aloud if this could be God's way of keeping her there despite her sense that it wasn't a good fit. She was more comfortable leading a small Bible study group that focused on the spiritual growth of the women themselves rather than leading in a parenting program. I told her that, of course, the women wanted her to stay—she was using her spiritual gift of exhortation. That didn't mean that this was the right ministry for her, however. She needed to find the sweet spot of her calling, including gifting and burden. MOPS wasn't the best fit for her life experience or her divine design.

Patricia was excited that although her spiritual gift was exhortation, she wasn't called to minister somewhere simply because others wanted her to do so. She was pleased to think that the phone calls she often received from other women could very well be a primary avenue of ministering encouragement. Instead of being involved where she didn't feel the joy of her calling, she began to recognize that the conversations God continued to send her way were an essential part of her personal ministry.

Discovering your Calling

Since your mission is your overarching purpose in God's kingdom, it is important that you discover what it is. That is why we will take two chapters to work through this topic. To find your calling, you will need to look at the intersection of three areas:

- Your divine design, including your spiritual gifts, your abilities, your life experiences, and your personality
- The burdens on your heart
- Your opportunities

We are now focused on your gifting or design. Once you contemplate how God has wired you, we will consider how that intersects with your burdens and opportunities to identify God's unique call on your life.

Your Divine Design

How has God designed you? What abilities do you have? They may be physical, mental, or gifts in art, music, or creativity. What life experiences have changed you and given you a special perspective? Are you people-oriented or task-oriented? Do you like details or do they bore you? Are you organized or not? Are you introverted (energized by time alone) or extroverted (energized by time with people)?

God has made you exactly the way that you are. Why is it then that so many of us want to be like someone else? Why do we long for other gifts, other abilities, and other personalities? Perhaps it is because we tend to see our own weaknesses and yearn for the strengths that are their polar opposites. Instead of being grateful for our gifts, too often we look around at others and seek to be someone whom we aren't. When I begin to try to be someone else, I remember Psalm 139, especially v. 14: "I will give thanks to Thee, for I am fearfully and wonderfully made" (NASB).

I am part introvert and part extrovert; I need both time with others and time alone. If my schedule is too packed either way, I begin to lose momentum and must reenergize by deliberately doing the opposite. Because of my wiring, I can be talkative and outgoing with friends, but I am also basically shy and reluctant to put myself in situations where I don't know anyone. I have always wanted to be able to carry on conversations with strangers and enjoy them, but I have never found a way to quite succeed. It's not who I really am.

But if I were extroverted and I got all of my energy from people, I wouldn't relish time alone writing Bible studies. God knew exactly what he was doing when he designed me as he did. I love women and enjoy ministering to them, but I can only do it so long until I need to be alone. My ministry has been a great mix of time with others and time by myself. Only God could have made me such a perfect fit!

Your Spiritual Gifts

> The one called by God to spiritual leadership can be confident that the Holy Spirit has given him or her all necessary gifts for the service at hand.[59]
>
> J. Oswald Sanders

God has great plans for you and for me. But he doesn't just push us out there and wish us good luck; he gives us everything we need in order to achieve the tasks that he asks us to do. I am so thankful for that truth. Your spiritual gifts are a big part of your divine design, and God has given each believer at least one of them to use for the benefit of the church.

What is a spiritual gift? It's a Spirit-given ability for service to the church; a *charismata*—a gift of grace. That tells us that it is not something we earn; it isn't given because of who we are. God bestows our gifts in spite of our sins and shortcomings so that we can benefit others.

> Now there are different gifts, but the same Spirit. And there are different ministries, but the same Lord. And there are different results, but the same God who produces all of them in everyone. To each person the manifestation of the Spirit is given for the benefit of all. For one person is given through the Spirit the message of wisdom, and another the message of knowledge according to the same Spirit, to another faith by the same Spirit, and to another gifts of healing by the one Spirit, to another performance of miracles, to another prophecy, and to another discernment of spirits, to another different kinds of tongues, and to another the interpretation of tongues. It is one and the same Spirit, distributing as he decides to each person, who produces all these things (1 Cor. 12: 4-11).

This passage outlines some basics about spiritual gifts:

+ The Spirit is behind them, revealing his presence.
+ He gives them to various people according to his choice, not ours.
+ He produces the results.
+ We have different gift sets and ministries.
+ Spiritual gifts are designed to benefit the church at large, not the individual.

Because we each work out of our giftedness and we all have different gifts, we should not expect others to think like we do or behave like we do. That tendency is gift imposition, insisting that everyone see and act through our gifts rather than recognizing that their gifts give them a different perspective. A friend's pastor demands that everyone in the congregation prioritize winning souls as he does as an evangelist. Another pastor with the gift of mercy can't understand why everyone isn't out there serving those who are hurting and unlovable. As a result, many in their congregations feel guilty that they cannot live up to such expectations.

Once I discovered my gift of teaching and began to enjoy digging into the Bible deeply, I thought that everyone would delight in the same thing if I could just show them how to do it. Was I wrong! My friends didn't always want to look up the Greek word or read a commentary about a passage. I was imposing my gifts on others while at the same time getting annoyed at those who did the same to me.

Not only can the 1 Corinthians passage help us recognize the viewpoints of others as valid, it can also help us avoid common confusion about spiritual gifts. They aren't the same as character (fruit of the Spirit), talents (natural abilities given at birth), or church offices (a pastor doesn't necessarily have the gift of pastoring). Instead, these are special abilities given by the Spirit at the point of trusting Christ to serve the church and to bring glory to God (Ephesians 4:12; 1 Corinthians 12:7; 1 Peter 4:10, 11).

Although we won't go into an in-depth study of spiritual gifts here, it is important to realize that God expects us to prioritize our time according to our giftedness.

> For by the grace given to me I say to every one of you not to think more highly of yourself than you ought to think, but to think with sober discernment, as God has distributed to each of you a measure of faith. For just as in one body we have many members, and not all the members serve the same function, so we who are many are one body in Christ, and individually we are members who belong to one another. And we have different gifts according to the grace given to us. If the gift is prophecy, that individual must use it in proportion to his faith. If it is service, he must serve; if it is teaching, he must teach; if it is exhortation, he must exhort; if it is contributing, he must do so with sincerity; if it is leadership, he must do so with diligence; if it is showing mercy, he must do so with cheerfulness (Rom. 12:3-8).

Here we are told to think discerningly, with honesty and insight from God about our gifts. Because they are bestowed by grace, they should not be a source of pride; neither should they be ignored. False modesty has no place in recognizing what God has given. Instead, we are to soberly consider them and serve others with them. Paul says that we are to use the gift of service by serving, to teach in the realm of teaching, and to use the gift of encouragement by encouraging. Basically, he exhorts us to focus our energies where our gifts are front and center. Instead of agreeing to serve because others ask, we are to be involved primarily in the area where our gifts lie.

Taking the Wind with You

I have been working out by riding a bicycle. Because my husband knows that I loved riding my bike as a girl, he suggested this as a form of exercise. (I've already tried a stationary bike, a gym, dance classes, running, walking, and the help of a trainer.) His intent was to refurbish our son's old mountain bike for me. However, before he got around to getting it down from the attic, our neighbor put her daughter's bike out for trash pickup. Knowing that I would prefer a lighter girl's model, he asked her if I could have it, and she was delighted to share it with us.

For the past few months, I have been riding around the neighborhood several times a week and have found that I actually enjoy it. I love being outside instead of in a gym; I appreciate opening the garage instead of having to go elsewhere to work out; I feel refreshed by nature; and best of all, I get to take the wind with me.

If you have ever lived in Texas or other places in the south, you probably know why I am excited about the wind. It gets very hot here during the middle of the summer, and that makes outdoor exercise very difficult on days when the air is still. On our hottest days in July and August, it can be ninety degrees by mid-morning. When I am on my bicycle, the wind goes with me because of speed. It's so much better than walking or running.

Serving God within the area of your gifting is like taking the wind with you. Instead of it being a chore and a bore, it is invigorating, a breath of fresh air into your life. That doesn't mean it's always easy; we may confront failure, lack of appreciation, or opposition. But there is a huge difference in trying to minister without the proper gift and serving through the power of the Spirit.

Years ago before I had even heard about spiritual gifts, I was involved in a young women's group at our church which seemed to me to be without much purpose. Our meetings were boring and, for the most part, fruitless. I felt that we needed a cause, some way to minister to others, and so I came up with a plan for us to visit our church members who lived in nursing homes. I got volunteers, made a schedule, and sent everyone out. The problem was that I was a terrible visitor for these poor folks! I had no clue what to talk about (remember, I said I am not outgoing); I was blank when it came to ways to practically assist them; and I simply wanted to leave. I don't have the gift of mercy and was absolutely terrible at trying to help others in such situations. At the time I didn't realize what the problem was, but I knew that I couldn't keep visiting the sick and aging.

What I recognized later was that I had used my gift of leadership to launch a needed ministry, but I lacked the gift to carry out the individual service. I wasn't a bad Christian for not being able to do this well; I was just misplaced. The wind simply wasn't with me.

Discovering your Spiritual Gifts

If you are to serve within your area of gifting, it is imperative that you discover your spiritual gifts as an essential element of your divine design. As you look for them, remember these guidelines:

+ You will enjoy serving when you use your gifts. (The wind will blow!)
+ Your gifts will be evidenced by fruit, although how much you reap is up to the Spirit.
+ Others will notice and provide confirmation. (I suggest that you avoid tests; they cannot provide real confirmation, which only comes from God and the watching eyes of mature believers.)
+ Try serving in a possible area of giftedness and see if you like it. Avoid long-term commitments until you are sure that it's the right spot for you.

Once you identify your particular spiritual gift set, you will need to consider how it pairs best with your natural gifting—personality, strengths, and weaknesses. In the next chapter we will take your divine design and incorporate your burdens and opportunities to help you determine where to serve to fulfill your mission. As Vickie Kraft has learned, "When you're following your calling there's great joy, satisfaction and fruit in doing so."[60]

In the Appendix is a spreadsheet of the spiritual gifts recorded in the Bible. Scholars are divided as to whether the Bible gives a comprehensive list of gifts or not. I have found, however, that when I consider the listed gifts in possible combinations and with an understanding of a person's nature and personality, I can explain and appreciate someone's strengths without suggesting additional gifts not mentioned in the New Testament.

If you have never studied these gifts, this is only a beginning point. Study the passages and the meanings of the words to help you identify your own gifting (Romans 12: 3-8; 1 Corinthians 12-14; Ephesians 4:7-16; 1 Peter 4:10-11).

You are on a great adventure as you move toward your calling. Your Personal Action Plan will help you along the way. Enjoy the journey!

Personal Action Plan

Chapter 4: Take the Wind with You

Assessment

God's call becomes clearer as you identify the intersection of your gifting, the desires of your heart, and your opportunities. As you discover how God has made you and what he has laid on your heart as burdens, you will begin to recognize the call that he has on your life—the particular mission for which he uniquely designed you! Once that happens, you should embrace that mission both in service and in further training as those opportunities arise. First, consider your divine design.

Spiritual gifting

The list below contains the spiritual gifts which are listed in New Testament passages (Romans 12:3-8; Ephesians 4:7-16; 1 Corinthians 12-14; 1 Peter 4:10-11). I have included a short definition of each in the Appendix of this book. Although these lists may not be comprehensive, you will have a good starting point for discovering your spiritual gifts. Consider the list prayerfully, asking God for insight. Refer back to the definitions on your chart and read the names in your translation. Mark the ones that are possibilities with a *question mark* and use a *star* for those that are certain.

Administration
Discernment of spirits
Exhortation
Faith
Giving
Interpretation of tongues
Leadership
Pastor-teacher
Teaching
Word of wisdom

Apostle
Performing miracles
Evangelist
Gifts of healings
Helps/Service
Kinds of tongues
Mercy
Prophecy
Word of knowledge

Talk to someone who knows you well and has seen you serving. Be sure it's a believer who knows something about spiritual gifting. Ask him or her for their thoughts about what gifts you may have and their reasoning. Mark those gifts on the above list with a **C** for confirmation if you already have it marked. If you don't, mark it with a *question mark* and the *friend's initials.*

How have these gifts been confirmed through fruit?

Other aspects of your divine design

There are many other facets of the way God has uniquely designed you. Consider anything else that comes to mind. Think through the questions below carefully, and then talk to others who know you well and can give you honest input.

Are you introverted (energized by time alone) or extroverted (energized by time with people)?

What abilities do you have? Think physical, mental, and gifts in art, music, or creativity.

Do you like details or do they bore you?

What other strengths do you possess?

Challenge

The only way to truly verify your spiritual gifting is to participate in ministry. Just because you teach school and may be comfortable in front of others or with children doesn't mean that teaching is your spiritual gift. Look for spiritual fruit from the ministry, not just training and comfort level.

Go back to your assessment. Of the spiritual gifts you have confirmed with a C, what possible areas of service would fit with your other abilities? Do you need to adjust where you are currently serving? Of the spiritual gifts that are possibilities, write down several ways to exercise them. In the next chapter we'll look at burdens and opportunities and put it all together. For now, simply write your ideas.

Support

Consider asking for support from someone who gave you input about your gifts. (If you are married, only ask for male support from your husband or a close relative so that you are wise in protecting your marriage; thus, I will assume from this point on that your support comes from a woman.) Ask your friend to pray for you during the time you work through the two chapters on calling. Tell her what ideas for service you have considered so that she can pray for wisdom for you and possibly help you think through the right fit.

Summary of my Plan:

My challenge(s):

My support in reaching this challenge:

CHAPTER 5

DO I HAVE TO GO TO AFRICA?
CALLING PART 2

Our calling involves everything we are and everything we do.[61]
Tullian Tchividjian

The summer after my sixth-grade year, my church youth group went to an encampment for a foreign missions conference. I don't remember a great deal about it, except that it was mostly boring, sometimes fun, and full of beauty in the New Mexico mountains. By the end of the week there, however, I was convinced that God had called me to foreign missions.

At that young age I associated such a call from God with going to Africa, and that scared me. Today I appreciate the youthful courage associated with my willingness, but I didn't really want to go. In that day travel wasn't so easy, and technology didn't allow for much communication with the United States. To go to Africa would take a huge leap of faith!

As I look back on it, I am not so sure that God ever designed me for Africa or any other foreign field; my experience on short-term trips has revealed my difficulty relating well with people in different cultures. Yet I do believe that God impressed me with a call to serve him at that young age, a call that all believers are to heed. But its particular look varies from person to person.

As noted in the previous chapter, finding your individual mission involves the intersection of these three things:

- Your divine design (spiritual gifts, abilities, experience, personality)
- Your burdens
- Your opportunities

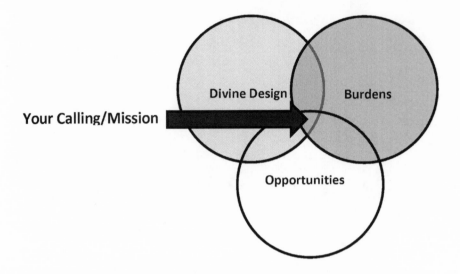

Hopefully, you have begun outlining your distinct design based on your spiritual, physical, and mental gifts, as well as your personality and life experience. All of these are bound up in your uniqueness. Once you discover your gifting, you have a responsibility to develop it over the course of time as God's steward. Taking time to do the Personal Action Plans give you a good start. After that, God will reveal your next step.

Burdens of your Heart

The second area that points to your calling involves the burdens you carry, not personal burdens but those for certain people or ministries. Some people call this area "passions" and others refer to it as "heart," but I prefer the word burdens. God has given you desires that accompany your mission; your calling will not be the last thing that you want to do. Although that should make some of you feel better about the possibility of being sent to Siberia for a lifetime, be aware that God does ask his followers to do things that are difficult or unwelcome because he is also developing their character. The point here, that burdens match the call, only concerns life mission, not every situation.

Once I realized that God wouldn't summon me to Africa without giving me the accompanying desire to go (unlike a short-term trip—think Jonah), I began to rest in his will for me. What or whom did I have on my heart? What bothered me? What did I want to fix in the world or the church? Such questions point to our personal burdens.

1 Corinthians 12:4-6 explains that God gives the gifts, the ministries, and the results. Our burdens help guide us to our specific ministries. For example, I have the gift of teaching but my ministry is to adults, primarily women. For some of you with teaching gifts, your ministry is focused on children or youth. My desire to see adults grounded in and living out the Scriptures directs me to my God-given area of service.

What does this burden look like? It may seem like passion or a concern for a particular group of people, a cause, a task, or need. It may surface because you see a lack somewhere. Ask yourself these kinds of questions:

+ To what people do I best relate and desire to help?
+ What bothers me?
+ What needs to be done?
+ What is essential?
+ What would I fix about the world, a situation, a group of people, or in the church if I could?

I discovered by elimination that God didn't call me to children. When I was forced to work with preschoolers monthly as a parent, I absolutely hated it. I love my own children very much and enjoyed having a few of their friends around at a time, but I immensely disliked being in charge of groups of young kids, and the bigger the group, the worse it was. Besides that, I found their activities boring. Every time I volunteered in the children's area, I counted the minutes until I could leave. After doing time in vacation Bible school for a couple of years, I began teaching women's Bible studies all summer long to escape that one week with the youngsters.

You may be able to eliminate a group similarly.

On the positive side, the things that bother me direct me toward my mission. A church with poor or absent Bible teaching disturbs me. Small groups that discuss their feelings without looking at the truths of God's Word seem pointless to me. Without good grounding in the Scripture, I feel that a church is failing in one of its primary tasks. In the same way, I notice when there is confusion about vision, lack of simple organization and coordination, and no defined objectives; such situations annoy me.

I also find that I am drawn to people with similar concerns. Likely because our gifting and calling are comparable, we have the same perspective and relate well. I learned from experience, however, that there is a danger in too much discussion among those who are zealous about a lack in their church. Often such conversations become counter productive when they focus on complaining rather than contributing to a solution. And I have to admit my own culpability in such murmuring.

You will need to consider how your burdens and passions intersect with your divine design. Finally, your opportunities help guide you to your personal mission.

Opportunities

There is no shortage of chances to serve, so we must be careful to make sure we take only those that fit our divine design and burdens.

When you are presented with a need, it is important to carefully pray about and analyze the opportunity. Consider these questions as you talk it over with God:

+ Is it in line with the way that God has been leading me and working through and with me in the past?
+ Does it fit my season in life?
+ Do I see God already at work in this opportunity?
+ Is it a kingdom-centered opportunity?

Spiritual Markers

The workbook *Experiencing God: Knowing and Doing the Will of God* really helped me understand the importance of reviewing the past. When God aligns a person with what he has called her to do, he consistently moves her in the general direction of her mission. Henry Blackaby suggests that we find God's will, in part, by writing down the spiritual markers we have experienced. These markers reflect times when God's specific call or direction was clear. [62] I think of these as road signs that point us the right way on our journey with God.

Just this past week I had time with some women, many of whom I have known for years. One friend remarked that I had been part of the lives of so many women who have gone on to lead others in some way; she mentioned herself and a number of other women who have sat under my teaching or leadership. When I left that conversation, I realized that she was commenting on a spiritual marker in my life that steered me in the direction of training leaders. That is a huge encouragement to me as I write this book, which is an extension of that mission. Such signposts confirm it as work I need to complete. For years I have been burdened that God's people be equipped to lead others well; the opportunity to equip others on a larger scale came when my time was freed to work on this book; and the markers confirm it as one aspect of my particular mission.

Life's Seasons

If the opportunity that presents itself doesn't suit your present season of life, it isn't part of your mission. As women, we must take into account our family circumstances. Although a situation may seem an exact fit, timing is everything.

A person's calling is consistent throughout life, but the way it plays out changes. Mine includes teaching the Scripture, which I have done in some form for thirty years. However, the specific ways that I have accomplished that have varied with my season of life. When my children were young, my teaching consisted of leading published Bible studies in my neighborhood. The groups were generally small; they were near my home; and the material was fairly basic. When I began leading Precept Bible studies[63] in my church, the groups were a bit larger, I spent more time driving to the location, and the studies required much more preparation. However, by then my daughter was in school full-time, and my son attended pre-school two mornings a week. My ministry further expanded during their school years as I was able to travel and teach leadership workshops for Precept Ministries. I didn't go to seminary or enter full-time ministry until my children were both in college. Because my husband traveled quite a bit with business and my kids were involved in a number of activities, a full-time ministry position was not a possibility for my family.

All along I was busy realizing my call to teach the Bible, but the way that worked out differed according to the season of my life and even my unique home situation. I learned somewhere along the way to get frequent input from my husband as to his perspective of how things were going. When people offered me any new responsibilities at church or my children's schools, we always agreed about them beforehand. Otherwise, I accepted our lack of agreement as a signal that the opportunity wasn't God's timing or perhaps not his will. My priorities were in this order: my relationship with God, my family, my ministry, and then a job. Putting family before ministry helped me recognize God's will by sifting out which opportunities were really from him.

In considering family as an important determining factor, I share the experience of a wise friend, Susie Hawkins:

> Just because we have an opportunity to minister does not mean it is God's will or God's best for us. A wise and

insightful leader will recognize that there are boundaries and scriptural principles that guide us as we decide where to invest our energies and values.

I learned this principle when I was serving on a church staff. My husband had left the pastorate to serve in a denominational position, which required a great deal of travel, especially preaching on the weekends. I had taken a staff position in women's ministry, which I had always enjoyed. As anyone knows, church work is all consuming! And it wasn't long before I realized we had a conflict between my needing to be at church on Sunday and my husband wanting me to travel with him on the weekends. A large part of his job was meeting other pastors and staff, and he wanted me to be with him (for which I am very thankful!). But it wasn't long until we realized that heading up two ministries in one marriage was not going to work for us. He was frustrated with me when I said I could not go with him due to sign-up for Bible study or special event meetings, etc. He couldn't understand why I couldn't get someone to fill in for me on a regular basis. While I could do that occasionally, I didn't feel that it was right for the ministry. And while he tried to be understanding, this became an ongoing tension in our marriage about which we began praying.

Finally, I decided to give up my position for two reasons: my first priority was my marriage and my husband and, secondly, the ministry I was leading deserved a leader who could give 100% to the work. As it turned out, this was the right decision, as I knew it would be. I continued to teach and serve on the leadership team; I just wasn't in charge of it all. It also enabled me to pursue something I had considered for several years but just couldn't find the time for – returning to school to study theology. That decision, which was wholeheartedly supported by my husband, was one of the best decisions I ever made. Theological education opened up a whole new world and was such a spiritual boost for me. I know now that I would probably never have been able to work on a master's degree if I had stayed on the church staff. In one sense it seemed as if my husband's desire for me to travel with him on the weekends limited my opportunities for church ministry. But on the other hand, it gave me valuable time with other ministry wives, not to mention pleasing him.

The opportunities we choose to take must be considered in the context of our marriage and family responsibilities. Marriage is designed for oneness, and God's best is for husband and wife to work together in agreement. Even if a husband is not a believer or not a strong believer, the wife can trust the Lord to use that principle to guide her decisions; if God is in it, the wife and husband will be united about the responsibilities that she assumes.

When family responsibility and ministry opportunity conflict, I always ask myself these questions: which of these responsibilities can be done only by me? Which can be done by someone else? Of course the answer is always the same—at least, so far! There are many other teachers, leaders, and speakers in the Christian world who can minister perfectly well. However, I am the only wife of my husband, mother of my daughters, grandmother of my grandkids and daughter of my aging mother. There will always be ministry opportunities, and there will be time for that in my future.[64]

Susie is blessed with a godly husband, but the principles she shares also apply when that is not the case. Our God has the power to turn any husband's heart to God's will, despite his failure to hear or even ask for God's input. The issue for us as wives is whether we trust God enough to believe that he will move mountains to make sure we do the work he has given us to accomplish. Nothing is impossible for God.

God at Work

In assessing which opportunities are God given, ponder whether God is already at work in the situation. This is more difficult to weigh because it is so subjective. Look for the little things that show God's hand. Were you already praying about such a situation when someone asked you to do it? Is there a link between the responsibility and your life experience? Generally, this guideline can only confirm once other criteria are met. Never take on service based on such subjectivity alone.

Kingdom Business

Remember that your mission is about the kingdom, not just your gifting or your burdens. The opportunity should move the kingdom forward in some way. The apostle Paul makes it clear that spiritual gifts are for the benefit of the church in 1 Corinthians 12. How does this responsibility move others toward the kingdom or move the church forward in its work? Choose commitments that advance the kingdom.

Focus your Life

Once you identify your calling through the intersection of divine design, burden, and opportunities, you are set free to focus your life instead of trying to do and be everything.

Do you feel overwhelmed with all that you have going on right now? The issue may be a failure to concentrate on God's mission. Instead of recognizing that his plans take priority over our plans, so often we fill our lives with other things—often very good things. If we eliminate the busyness that doesn't contribute to God's call on our lives, we can truly focus and simplify our lives. We see this biblically in the lives of Jesus and Paul.

Like Jesus

When people around him wanted Jesus to do their will instead of God's, he refused. "And when day came, He departed and went to a lonely place; and the multitudes were searching for Him, and came to Him, and tried to keep Him from going away from them. But He said to them, 'I must preach the kingdom of God to the other cities also, for I was sent for this purpose'" (Luke 4:42-43, NASB).

Later, when faced with a cruel death, rejection, and heartache, Jesus resolved to head to Jerusalem, knowing what would happen as essential to his mission: "Now when the days drew near for him to be taken up, Jesus set out resolutely to go to Jerusalem" (Luke 9:51).

Despite the fact that Jesus failed to heal everyone, save everyone, or meet all the needs of others, at the end of his life he was able to say, "I glorified you on earth by completing the work you gave me to do" (John 17:4).

We, too, must determine to fulfill our God-given calling. That means there will be things left undone around us, things that God isn't calling us to do. We have to walk so closely with him that we recognize the difference and act accordingly.

Like Paul

Paul exemplified the same type of focus on God's mission. When he described his conversion experience to King Agrippa, he reported how Jesus had defined his calling:

> The Lord replied, "I am Jesus whom you are persecuting. But get up and stand on your feet, for I have appeared to you for this reason, to designate you in advance as a servant and witness to the things you have seen and to the things in which I will appear to you. I will rescue you from your own people and from the Gentiles, to whom I am sending you to open their eyes so that they turn from darkness to light and from the power of Satan to God, so that they may receive forgiveness of sins and a share among those who are sanctified by faith in me" (Acts 26:15-18).

Paul kept this mission in mind throughout his life. In his final letter written shortly before his execution, he noted that he had fulfilled it:

> For I am already being poured out as a drink offering, and the time of my departure has come. I have fought the good fight, I have finished the course, I have kept the faith; in the future there is laid up for me the crown of righteousness, which the Lord, the righteous Judge, will award to me on that day; and not only to me, but also to all who have loved His appearing (2 Timothy 4:6-8, NASB).

Although Paul finished God's assigned work, he left a lot of things undone, choosing to concentrate on what Jesus commissioned him to do—teaching and preaching the gospel to the Gentiles.

When we center our lives around our individual missions, as Jesus and Paul did, we must let some other opportunities and activities go. If we understand that God empowers us where he sends us, we realize that focusing on our callings maximizes our influence. I do more to affect others when I am about the work that God has specifically designed me to do than when I am doing anything else, as good as it may be.

In general, we decline opportunities outside our calling. They may be wonderful places to serve; they may have huge needs; but they are there for someone whose mission matches. In contrast, we agree to those openings that suit our unique calling.

When I am offered a place to serve, I look at my mission to see if the responsibility is in line with my gifting, experience, and burden. If not, I don't accept it. Calling helps prioritize the way I spend my time.

Applying this may involve something small, like saying no to cooking dinner for a new mom, or it can mean choosing to invest my time studying to teach rather than going door-to-door to evangelize. Once I began working full-time on a church staff, I realized that I could no longer take meals every time there was a cry for help; I also knew that God had plenty of other women available, and he didn't need me.

At this point you may be thinking that your present working situation isn't conducive to your mission. You may find yourself in a position that doesn't quite fit your gifting, yet you are stuck there because of circumstances beyond your control. Instead of thinking "job" when you consider focusing on your calling, think influence. How does your mission to influence the world intersect with the position you hold? Are there people there who need your encouragement and spiritual discernment? How can you fulfill your calling where you already are? God's kingdom plans may require you to be employed where you don't find happiness, where there is not a great fit for your gifting and burdens. A sense of purpose may come, however, when you learn to see every circumstance as your opportunity to complete your mission. Look for those opportunities and watch God at work.

Hindrances to Focusing on Mission

So why don't we focus our influence as Jesus and Paul did? It sounds easy, but most of us fail at this consistently, even when we have identified our individual missions. What distracts us from our focus?

Pleasing People

Often we women take responsibility because we hate to hurt or disappoint someone else. Paul had this to say about pleasing people: "Am I now trying to gain the approval of people, or of God? Or am I trying to please people? If I were still trying to please people, I would not be a slave of Christ!" (Galatians 1:10). We must determine in advance whom we want to please or we will find ourselves distracted from the tasks that we should be doing, those that advance our God-given missions.

Desire for Recognition/Advancement

Unfortunately, an awareness of God's unconditional love doesn't stop us from seeking notice and recognition. Jesus said, "Beware of practicing your righteousness before me to be noticed by them; otherwise you have no reward with your Father who is in heaven" (Matthew 6:1, NASB). If you feel drawn to a position because it makes you feel good about yourself, ask God for insight into your own heart and the grace to face your pride or your need. God alone, not a position or a calling, is to be the source of our fulfillment.

Guilt

As we read earlier, when the crowds approached Jesus demanding that he stay with them, he focused on his mission instead of giving in to guilt. Instead, we often do just the opposite. For example, have you ever agreed to serve children when the need was announced, knowing you have other gifts or that God hasn't called you to children? If so, you likely took time away from things you are supposed to do and robbed the person called to such tasks of the joy of ministry.

Keeping Up with the Culture

Our culture makes its own demands. When we think our kids must be active in every sport, our houses must look like showplaces, or everything must be perfect for company or our neighbors, we lose time, energy, effort, and money needed for God's kingdom. It really is okay to say no to the dictates of our overly goal-oriented and perfectionistic culture.

Busyness

Busyness parallels cultural demands, but it may also involve failure to implement biblical priorities. We may be too busy because our careers have pulled us off track from God's best. Perhaps we seek money, success, control, or any number of worldly things rather than God's kingdom. It may be that we have accepted the mindset that our families need constant entertainment rather than refreshment in low-key time together. Jesus warned us to seek first God's kingdom and his righteousness over our basic needs (Matthew 6:25-34). When we ask God for direction with our time, we must assess our motives and purposes. Simplifying life depends upon focused priorities.

Failure to Deal with the Past

Working through our issues is essential for moving forward and refocusing from ourselves to others. Ask God to help you carefully search your heart for bitterness, unforgiveness, negative patterns, and wrong thinking. Make sure that your marriage is strong and healthy. Seek wise counsel for help in moving beyond such issues. It is impossible to serve others well until we deal with the problems that weigh us down.

As you consider your calling, take time to ask God if you are guilty of allowing any of these distractions to keep you from fulfilling the mission that he has given you.

Life Out of Balance or In Balance?

In order to accomplish our individual missions, our lives will be out of balance. Jesus' life was; Paul's was. We aren't called to a balanced life but to a life of purpose. It is impossible to have real balance in the sense of doing everything equally and also fulfill God's call. I certainly can't do it; there are some things that just don't fit into my schedule right now. In order to complete my mission, I must say no to many worthwhile activities and tasks. Although we women like to think we can have it all, we really can't, at least not all at the same time.

On the other hand, if we think of balance in the sense of navigating our priorities well, that is a goal we need to pursue. It is a balancing act to learn how to spend quality time with God, love our family, fulfill our God-given calling, and care for ourselves so that we persevere. Learning to decline invitations to serve outside of our gifting helps prevent overload, but there is a continual need to take each day's schedule to God for direction and priority.

Katie Brazelton, who wrote *Pathway to Purpose for Women* says, "God's purpose will cost you your life in the sense that you must choose to die to self and accept his plan. It will cost you your life, too, in that you will be spent and used up in service to God. It will stretch you to such an impossible degree that you will fail without Him."[65]

Writing a Mission Statement

One great way to stay focused on your life purpose is to actually write a personal mission statement. Having such a document handy will remind you of your kingdom priorities. Here are some guidelines to help you.

It is a Process

Don't expect to write your mission statement in an hour or a day; it is a process, and the process is valuable. Don't feel that you must finish it within a particular time frame, but work through it slowly, carefully praying about it. Give yourself the grace to listen to God and to others who know you well.

Keep it Short

Making your statement short forces you to think through it very carefully. The first draft that I wrote was too long and involved too much. Succinct verbiage also makes it easier to remember. If you are easily distracted from your life purpose by other things, knowing it by heart will help you quickly determine when to say no.

Use Scripture or Biblical Concepts that Apply

Including scripture isn't necessary, but you may find it very helpful. This doesn't involve quoting an entire verse but pulling out a phrase. Using God's words is a reminder that your calling has a kingdom objective in line with God's work in the world. Some scriptural concepts may be helpful— words like grace, serve, love, sacrifice, teach, build up, minister, gospel, or encourage.

Laurie Beth Jones, author of *The Path*, gives a formula for writing a mission statement, which you may find helpful, as I did:

> My mission is to _____, _____, and _____ (fill in with 3 verbs that fit you) _____ (a core value such as service, justice, mercy, truth, freedom, etc.) to, for, or with _____ (this is the group or cause that most excites you).[66]

I used her suggested outline as the basis of my own statement, but you can see that it is a loose connection. This is the latest version: "My mission is to teach God's Word, to train godly leaders, and to give vision and simplicity to ministry so that others are challenged to grow as vessels for God's use in the world."

Moving Out on Mission when God Calls

Knowing your calling frees you to say no to extraneous activities and focus on the things that God has designed you to do, maximizing your influence on others and enjoyment of the task. Rather than hurry to complete this Personal Action Plan, work through it prayerfully, carefully, and with due deliberation. Once you identify your calling, make the tough choices required to focus your life in that direction.

Although fulfilling God's mission is often difficult, I have found that following God's calling is the most exciting place to be in life. As you move forward with your mission, you will be blessed as well!

Personal Action Plan

Chapter 5: Do I Have to Go to Africa?

Assessment

By way of review, you are searching for the intersection of your divine design, your burdens, and your opportunities. Review your Personal Action Plan from Chapter 4.

Burdens

Do you have a passion for a particular group of people (*i.e.*, kids, women, immigrants), a cause, a task, or a need? If so, explain the desires of your heart in that regard.

What lack do you see in the church globally or locally? Another way to ask this is to think about what bothers you. What needs to be done by the church? What would you consider essential for the church to be about? What weaknesses or omissions bother you?

What would you fix about (or do to help) the world, a group of people, or the church if you could?

What ministry would you undertake if there were no obstacles?

Consider how your desires and burdens intersect with your gifting. Write down your insights at this point of your search to discover or confirm your calling/mission.

Opportunities

In what ministry are you presently involved? Why?

Write out the spiritual markers of your life. Prayerfully think of times when God has clearly led you. Consider how they line up and point you to God's calling or mission.

What opportunities matching your gifts and burdens are open to you in your local church? If you are uncertain, whom can you ask?

How does your season of life intersect with those opportunities?

How have you seen God already at work to move you in this direction?

What obstacles would prevent you from participating in those opportunities right now? Are they obstacles that force you to "wait on God" or are they obstacles of your own making that need to be overcome? Explain your answer.

Hindrances

Spend some time with God, asking him which hindrances below are keeping you from focusing on his mission. Mark those that apply to you.

Pleasing people
Desire for recognition/advancement
Guilt
Keeping up with the culture
Busyness
Failure to deal with your past

Challenge

What is your plan to use your gifts as they intersect with your desires and opportunities? You may already be fulfilling your mission. If so, write down what you do and how you have confirmed it; then consider how you can challenge yourself to grow in the areas of your calling. Write down your thoughts.

Calling/mission statement

Part of your challenge is to think through what you learn about your calling/ mission so that you can clearly see what opportunities square with that mission and which ones don't. Once you begin to identify your gifts, desires, and opportunities, begin working on a personal mission statement. Write down your first draft below and continue to work on it as you read this book and as you discover more about how God made you.

Support

E-mail the person supporting you in your search to discover your call. What do you need in the way of accountability from her? Be specific in your goals. Talk to her about the hindrances with which you specifically deal. Return the favor by contacting her regarding her areas of need or accountability. Write down how you will find support for your action plan and from whom you will receive it.

Summary of my Plan:

My challenge(s):

My support in reaching this challenge:

CHAPTER 6

BAA! BAA! CARE

Shepherding . . . begins with a compassionate heart for individual sheep.[67]

Timothy S. Laniak

Care, the fourth fundamental of leadership, involves obeying Jesus' command to "love your neighbor as yourself" (Mark 12:31).

God calls people sheep, which implies that we require much care. Although I love the pastoral picture of sheep on a hillside, I don't particularly enjoy being compared to animals that are considered rather dumb and completely defenseless. (Studies have proven them to be as smart as cattle.[68] I wonder—does that make them smart?) Without the shepherd's care, sheep get lost, become easy prey, and die of hunger or disease. I may like to think that I am not as stupid as sheep, but I must admit that without Christian community, I easily fall into the same kinds of situations spiritually that they do physically. I need care just as you do, just as those whom you influence do.

Apparently, sheep require nourishment, protection from predators, and leadership to safe and nutritious environments.[69] Thus, the shepherd's care includes guiding, protecting, and providing for his flock out of love and concern for their welfare.

Two common biblical images for God are shepherd and father; both roles require protective care. The Scriptures also compare him to a mother, a gardener, and a husband. Such illustrations help facilitate our understanding that God is attentive to our needs. Take a few minutes to consider verbs or adjectives that describe the concern suggested by these images. Meditate on each one, pondering the emotions they evoke. As an example to spur your thinking, I would choose the verb "nurture," which makes me feel content and safe.

God calls his people to meet the needs of other sheep, as seen in the many "one another" commands in the New Testament, the picture of the church as a body and Jesus's example. Old Testament leaders are called shepherds of the nation, and the New Testament refers to the elders of the church in the same way. Clearly, care is essential in leading others.

Not only does the Bible emphasize the need to love those whom we influence, but even secular leadership material stresses its importance. One book based on military leadership principles puts it this way: "A leader cares that the job gets done—and he or she cares about the people doing the job."[70]

A shepherd who fails to tend his sheep will eventually lose his flock, which will become lost, scattered, injured, and sick. In the same way, influence fades quickly when a woman doesn't practically love the individuals that she attempts to lead.

I Said "Baa!"

I wonder if my young adult years of wandering spiritually could have been averted by the love and care of a good shepherd. No one outside of my own family ever reached out to mentor me or to disciple me. Because I felt left out and alone even in the midst of church involvement, I began to stray unnoticed. Although I appeared as a contented sheep on the outside, my mind was considering other paths. Those who were supposed to shepherd and influence me—my Sunday school teachers, my youth ministers, older girls in my youth group—never developed a close enough relationship with me to discover how I was personally doing in my walk with Christ.

Nevertheless, God cared for me himself and led me back to his flock. There I developed relationships with Christians who took a personal interest in me. When they challenged me to grow spiritually, I responded because of the care they lavished on me.

Think about people who have most influenced you—parents, teachers, friends, or leaders of other kinds. How have they cared for you? How have they shown their love? How did that affect your choice to listen to them?

Shepherds Know their Sheep

Jesus described himself as the Good Shepherd, saying, "He calls his own sheep by name and leads them out" (John 10:3). Because Christ knows us individually and personally, he is aware of our needs, our desires, our weaknesses, and our sins. Thus, he understands how to guide, protect, and provide for our true needs.

In the same way, you must personally get to know those whom you lead, and that requires an investment of time. They may be sheep already in God's flock or those who need to trust the Good Shepherd for salvation. Either way, only by personal attention can you discover how to best care for each individual whom you influence. (This cannot be done exclusively online by e-mails or text; it requires face-to-face interaction as much as possible. So many women are desperate for bonds, and these are impossible to develop without time together.)

Carmen Renee Berry shares three things which women seek in a church:

+ *Acceptance*—I don't want to be excluded because I'm not at the same place in my life's journey as you are.
+ *Understanding*—Be willing to get to know me because I have hurts and needs that have brought me here.
+ *Contribution*—A place where I can work with a circle of friends toward growing and serving.[71]

Apparently, the sequence is important. Women are looking for a church that will care about (in this order) "where I am, what I need, and how I can contribute."[72] It is essential to provide the same things for those whom you want to lead spiritually. First, accept them in love despite your feelings about their lifestyles or beliefs; second, learn about their hurts and needs and provide care; and third, help them understand that their friendship is important and meaningful to you—that it brings value to your life. Involve them as you serve others.

Many women develop through relationships, an important aspect of their learning and decision-making.[73] Thus, relationships are primary in leading them to follow Christ. Seek to deepen your understanding of who they are and what they need through open-ended questions:

+ Ask about feelings. Examples: How do you feel about your job? What is valuable to you about family? What is your greatest daily challenge? What is important to you about your children?
+ Ask about their core values, what they believe in, what makes them feel alive, what they care deeply about.
+ Listen, listen, and listen again to their answers.[74]

Just as Jesus took time with his followers, we must be available to interact with those whom we influence so that we come to know them and their needs.

Providing Nourishment and Healing

> Sheep will follow the shepherd who personally provides, protects, and guides.[75]
>
> Timothy S. Laniak

I have learned that a leader's practical care motivates others to follow her. My own small groups flourished when I spent time caring for the women involved. I watched other leaders struggle when they failed to take time to provide for the physical and emotional needs of their groups.

Nancy Fowler has been a mentor in the MOPS[76] program for several years. She carefully tailors the specific ways that she cares for those in her small group to the unique needs of the women: "Young moms are often overwhelmed with life in general and a kind word via phone, e-mail or text is so well received. One time I spent the morning helping with Christmas decorating. The mom was so delighted to have the help, and we had a good bonding time. Other times we meet for lunch, dinner, or coffee. Time away with another adult is huge for them."[77]

As she has grown in understanding their needs, she has discovered other critical ways to care. "In this ministry, I find that being interested in their kids is just about as important to them as interest in themselves! I often get down on the level with their preschoolers to visit with them. I've found when you care about their children it is like caring for the mom's heart as well."[78]

Nancy recognizes that young moms need relationships with other adults, relief from constant duties at home, and loving influences on their children. Clearly, she unselfishly gives her time to her flock, but she enjoys the relationships, too. What may seem like a sacrifice results in blessings for both women.

Psalm 23 pictures God providing for all of our needs, both physical and emotional:

> The Lord is my shepherd,
> I shall not want.
> He makes me lie down in green pastures;
> He leads me beside quiet waters.
> You have anointed my head with oil. (vv. 1-2, 5, NASB)

I love the way this beloved psalm pictures the shepherd supplying the needs of his sheep by leading them to lush pastures and still water, places where they will not encounter poisonous food and drink. They lie down in contentment and rest because they are full and healthy. The shepherd puts oil on their heads (v.5) to keep flies out of their hair.[79] He furnishes food, rest, and health for his sheep.

In what ways do we tend to those in our circle of influence? I have given meals, food, money, clothing, shelter, and transportation to others in times of sickness or hardship. Other believers have supplied for me in the same ways.

Periodically more is required, and Jesus's example convicts me: "I am the good shepherd. The good shepherd lays down his life for the sheep" (John 10:11). There are situations that involve more than a meal or two in order to love as Jesus loves, times when we must die to ourselves. Mary Anderwald describes such a situation:

> Some time ago at a staff meeting at the ministry where I work, our boss encouraged us to be shepherds to the people with whom God leads us to mentor and work. He said that might very well mean having them live with us, mentioning my extra room. Within days I had a voice mail from Brenda, whom I haven't seen in several years. She needed help for a friend whose husband was kicking her out. I went to Bible study that evening, thinking I would deal with this matter later. That night, the leader asked us to bow in prayer and tell God whether we were going to surrender to his will in our lives or not. Immediately, that phone call went through my mind and I prayed. The next morning in my regular telephone prayer time with a friend, I told her about the situation and she prayed that God would show me very clearly beyond a shadow of doubt what his will was in this matter.
>
> When I arrived at work the next morning, I found that I had received a devotional from the leader of our ministry based on Romans 12:1-14. Verse 13 jumped off the page at me: "Contribute to the needs of the saints and seek to show hospitality," (ESV). At this point I decided to return Brenda's phone call. She explained that this couple

was being evicted from their apartment. Although the husband had found a new place to live, he decided to take only their eighteen-year-old son with him. He told his wife that she could not go with them as "he just did not feel it anymore."

When I finally called the lady, she told me that she had made arrangements to go to a shelter, but she would be required to be out between 8 a.m. and 5 p.m. each day. The distance between the shelter and her part-time job was quite far. I agreed to talk to our employment services people to see if they could help her find a full-time position. Well, of course, all I could think about was the fact that she would be homeless and on the streets during the day when she wasn't at work. I was neither contributing to her needs nor showing hospitality. I knew that I would have no peace if I didn't give her a place to live.

As I write this, I have a housemate working part-time, looking for a full-time job. I don't know how this story will end. I believe that I am there to be a spiritual influence on her while I minister to her very real physical needs. I am waiting to see how God writes the rest of the story. But for now, he and I are feeding a very hungry woman and I have crammed everything that was in my guest room into my closet. I don't like to live with other people, but I know I am in his will by doing so![80]

To discern when to step into such a position, we must walk closely with God, listening for his voice as Mary did. She was wise not to take in someone totally unknown, but one with whom she shared a mutual friend. God won't lead us to such a level of care unless he makes it very clear. I appreciate the way that Mary continued asking and seeking to be absolutely sure this was God's direction. Instead of agreeing out of guilt, she carefully judged a number of circumstances and conversations. Extreme care situations such as this require great wisdom, and Mary sought counsel from others.

The power of God's Spirit is available to enable us to love this selflessly. All he asks from us is the willingness to die to our own selfishness in order to care for others, particularly those whom we already influence or hope to lead spiritually. He will guide us daily in the specifics of that provision. We can know that when he calls us to sacrificial care, he will deliver the means and the strength to follow through.

Jesus is the Good Shepherd of those who will come to believe in him (John 10:16). Just as he reached out to provide for those not yet following him, we must do the same. When we show practical love to others, we bring his kingdom to them in a real way. Such service opens their ears to hear about the Savior who loves them. By caring for a stranger, my friend Jody Curran and her husband were able to become lifelong spiritual mentors:

> About thirty years ago as a fairly new believer, my brother asked me to pray for, contact, and encourage a man in his Bible study in the local prison. As a result, I began writing and visiting Daryl. (It was a little daunting to stand in line at the prison with so many people waiting to see their kids or mates!) Daryl could hardly read and was struggling to write to me. After he accepted Jesus as his Savior, he really began to grow.
>
> Daryl ended up serving twenty-three years, and we kept in touch. In my letters I shared my story of coming to faith and my own struggles with life and circumstances. We sent books, tracts, and money for supplies. I watched him grow in his faith in really trying circumstances. He sang and played guitar in the prison choir, helped the chaplain, and had a good record.
>
> I went to a parole hearing after about twenty years. The parole board not only denied his plea, but they were also cruel and unkind to him. However, I will never forget his response after being denied parole: "I reckon the Lord wants me here longer to tell those young guys coming through not to waste their lives behind those bars."
>
> He was released just after the devastation of Hurricane Katrina, and his only family left in New Orleans was one brother. We picked him up at midnight and brought him home with us. He was with us for four months as we helped him get a driver's license, register to vote, look for

work and learn how to navigate a world that had changed dramatically in twenty-three years with computers and cell phones. It was like having a ten-year-old again who required a lot of patience and direction.

He first got a part-time job at a local grocery store and also landed a job as an apprentice in a company that produces and installs aluminum duct work for big commercial properties. He has kept both jobs for the past four years. He plays in the church band at three local churches. He comes by often to borrow some tools or celebrate a family birthday, Christmas or Thanksgiving. He is family and we love him. And he's a true testimony to God's grace. He's blessed our lives by seeing what God can do when we're willing to step out of our comfort zone and help.[81]

Jody's story is a wonderful example of giving what is needed to bring someone to health—physically and spiritually. Just like Mary, Jody was careful and wise when she took in Daryl. By then she had known him over twenty years and had been able to witness his repentance and changed life. Yes, Jody and her husband sacrificed for Daryl, but it was a joy for them to help him begin a new life, not an obligation.

God asks all of us to care as Jesus did—sacrificially. However, what we give up will be unique to our situations. Few of us will have someone live with us. Our sacrifices are more likely to involve time, perhaps our most precious possession, or befriending someone difficult to love.

Providing for the sheep involves ministering to their brokenness as well as their physical needs. As sinful people in a damaged world, we all experience hurts that may leave us unable to care for ourselves. God promised to shepherd Israel when their leaders failed to do so: "I will seek the lost, bring back the scattered, bind up the broken and strengthen the sick. . ." (Ezekiel 34:16, NASB). Just as the shepherd sees to the health of his sheep, we must attend to the emotional and spiritual needs of others.

I have to admit my inadequacies in providing emotional healing for others. I feel incompetent, knowing that other women are better suited and more experienced in meeting such needs. However, I can be a good listener and ask pertinent questions to help me know individuals. Hopefully, my attention and concern in conversation and prayer reflect my love and are the keys to my care. I make it a point to ask for updates on life situations, heartaches, feelings, and needs shared with me. The hurts of others become my own hurts—and that is the heart of a leader. "Rejoice with those who rejoice, and weep with those who weep" (Rom. 12:15, NASB).

I love Beverly Hislop's list of what women in pain need to know:

+ I am not alone—listen to my story
+ My feelings matter—empathize with me
+ There is hope—reflect my options
+ I can move forward—respect my choices[82]

When I hear of terrible hurts experienced by so many women, I feel helpless and want to draw back rather than reach toward them. That is why I so appreciate this practical list to guide my caring response. I can realistically listen; I can be compassionate; I can give hope; and I can allow a woman to make her own decisions. If someone needs more intense counseling or assistance than I can supply, I can offer prayer and help her find support.

I regularly enlist others to meet specific needs when I cannot. If long-term counseling is necessary, I refer people to those whose experience and calling enable them to assist. When someone's illness necessitates physical aid, I do what I can but I also recruit others—her small group, the church at large, or governmental and para-church and local agencies which are purposed to deal with such issues. (Just to be clear, that doesn't mean that I never do things, but I do find assistance for ongoing or specialized care.)

While on church staffs, I focused the majority of my care on my leadership circle and expected them to provide for those under them. If each woman attends to those closest to her, such circles should reach everyone connected to the body of Christ. On the other hand, our contacts outside the church body may need more time and personal care if they have no other support system.

Protecting the Sheep

Not only do sheep need a shepherd to keep them fed and healthy, they need her protection. The shepherd's rod is his primary weapon (Psalm 23:4). Without natural defenses, sheep are totally dependent upon the shepherd to keep predators away.

As we love and care for those whom we influence, we discover the weaknesses and vulnerabilities which make them easy targets for their spiritual enemy, Satan. The Scriptures warn about his attacks: "Be sober and alert. Your enemy the devil, like a roaring lion, is on the prowl looking for someone to devour" (1 Peter 5:8). Paul cautions the Ephesians to be prepared to battle his forces: "Clothe yourselves with the full armor of God so that you may be able to stand against the schemes of the devil. For our struggle is not against flesh and blood, but against the rulers, against the powers, against the world rulers of this darkness, against the spiritual forces of evil in the heavens" (Ephesians 6:11-12).

Whether we influence our children or a co-worker, it is imperative that we watch for signs that the enemy is encroaching into their thinking and behavior. As protectors, we must pray for them and speak the truth in love to them (Ephesians 4:15). Sometimes that involves honestly confronting other believers when they sin (Matthew 18:15-16; Galatians 6:1-2). If you are like me, this is the last thing that you want to do! It does help to remember that by speaking the truth in love, we defend them against the enemy and the consequences of their own sins. (When a woman is not a believer, confronting her is not appropriate. Instead, she needs to run to the Savior for salvation. She cannot escape sin's hold on her without the power of Christ.)

As a leader, I have challenged Christians on a number of occasions. Once, a woman involved in our Bible study leadership spoke harshly to the coordinator, whom we'll call Betsy, saying that no other leaders liked her or wanted to work with her. She indicated that her comments were based on a lunch conversation with a number of them. Of course, Betsy was crushed and came to me ready to resign her position. I convinced her to stay, but I had to deal with the gossip and murmuring within the group. I realized that all of them didn't comment about Betsy, but they also didn't publically disagree.

As I met with each woman individually, I made it clear that I wasn't asking who made the comments because they were all wrong to enter into it or to allow such gossip and murmuring to continue. I expected them as leaders to stop it in the future because it was judgmental and harmful. Although I dreaded each and every conversation, they went very well, and all the women expressed sorrow for their complicity. By making them aware of scriptural ways to deal with complaints or gossip, I helped protect them from disunity and sin.

In another situation, I had to ask a woman not to attend our Bible study until she dealt with her unforgiveness. At the time she was furious at her leader, refusing to speak to her despite the leader's confession of wrongdoing.

Yet, she insisted on attending the small group. As an angry and unforgiving woman, she didn't respond well to the boundary I set. Allowing her to be unforgiving and letting her spread that poison among other women would not have been the loving thing to do, however, for her or anyone else who may have been affected. I loved her enough to ask her to forgive her leader and reconcile with her. I tried to protect her from the devil who desires to create bitterness and disunity. Although she was unwilling to listen initially, in time she softened and reestablished relationships with us both.

Protecting others can be a difficult and even dangerous task because they don't always appreciate the truth; therefore, we risk losing or alienating friends. However, Jesus cared enough to confront those who were headed the wrong way, and he calls us to do the same. When the situation demands speaking the truth in love, don't rush but spend much time with God who can give you the words you need. As a shepherd, you must protect those who are vulnerable and defenseless.

By this point you may find yourself fearful of reaching out to others because such relationships may involve difficult care. Yet that is what we are called to do from time to time. Some people are better gifted to deal with very hard people. For the rest of us, such situations force us to rely upon the guidance and power of God's Spirit, as well as the wisdom of experienced believers. I have often consulted with counselors, other ministers, or leaders in recovery programs when I find myself lost as to how to protect a defenseless sheep. Use the resources that God has placed in your church or contact a para-church ministry that specializes in the area of need. You may not avoid the hard conversation, but you can go into it more prepared.

Guiding the Sheep

Shepherds not only provide health and protection, but they also offer guidance for the sheep.

My friend, whom we'll call Martha, seems to attract women who go astray without godly guidance. They struggle to apply scriptural principles to their own lives. Even when they know the truth, they don't follow it. Through the years that I have known her, I have observed Martha continue to love and guide such women, even though they may reject her advice. She shares one such story:

> God's ideas about caring and mine can be very different.
> He brings women into my life that I would never meet

otherwise. Some come for a relatively short period, and others are around for years and a deep bond forms as we walk together through her trials.

My husband and I met weekly with Melissa and Jim from our church for over a year trying to work out the issues that were tearing the marriage apart. She had been working on her own issues for a while and was beginning to make changes through recovery meetings. Her husband did not see that he needed to change—if she would just change everything would be okay. We continued our meetings long after it was evident that he was not going to change because Melissa needed our support. It is really hard to keep walking with someone who doesn't want to change and/or doesn't see the need to change his/her own behavior. Finally, we told them that we could no longer meet with them as a couple unless Jim implemented our counsel.

I continued to meet with Melissa for another six months or so, and she decided to file for divorce. Life got really ugly—court hearings and false custody charges that took her children away from her. Caring for someone can take you into some uncomfortable situations.

When the divorce was final, she began dating another man. My cautions were not taken and she married him. In caring I had to be willing to step back and let her go without getting my feelings hurt or getting angry so I could be there for the next chapter. I hoped that this would be a healthy marriage. It was not; it was verbally and emotionally abusive. Of course, it did not last long. I was so sad to see her "jump out of the frying pan and into the fire." My job was to love her and not let my feelings and admonitions get in the way. I walked with her until she got her feet back on the ground.

The Lord was with me teaching me and answering my "arrow prayers." I had to learn to accept rejection and be okay when my wisdom and experience were not taken. I had to let go of her "stuff" so I could be with my own family—sometimes that is really hard when you care about someone and are hurting with them. Another hard part was learning not to do what she needed to do for herself. I needed to limit phone calls. I had to keep my mouth shut so she could hear herself. Sometimes I had to say, "When you tell the same stories over and over it keeps you in the grip of the problem and builds resentment." I wanted her to get into the solution, "What can you do about that?" There were times that I had to send "arrow prayers" to help me show grace and to be sensitive to her fear and hurt.

These care-relationships seem to be one of God's ways of teaching me about boundaries, compassion, healthy caring, as well as mirroring areas where I need to work on myself.[83]

I so appreciate Martha's words about boundaries. Although we care, we cannot make others accept our advice, even when it is straight out of Scripture. What we can do is entrust the individuals to God.

Placing the Sheep in the Care of the Good Shepherd

Whatever a person's needs involve, we must be faithful to pray and place her in the hands of the true shepherd of our souls, God himself.

Now that sounds easy, but my tendency is to tell God how to fix the person's problems or to tell her how to fix herself, usually because I want to her free from difficulties. Instead, I have learned that it is better to pray kingdom prayers and to leave the specifics in the hands of a loving and all-knowing God. What is a kingdom prayer? It is one that prays "thy kingdom come" for the situation.

A number of years ago, someone asked me to pray for her husband, who wasn't a Christ-follower. Her request was that God would send him more business during a slow period which had greatly affected their income. Although I heard no voice, it was as if God said to me, "What if I need him to struggle to bring him to faith?" I realized that I often prayed opposite God's will by focusing on what I thought people needed instead of what he might be doing on a kingdom level. Once I recognized this, I revised many of my prayers, concentrating them on seeing God's kingdom come in the person's heart instead of praying for her ease, success, physical health, house sale, or happiness. Of course, I still ask God to move in miraculous ways, but I focus more on what he wants to do with her and through her in the midst of illness or difficulty.

Consider these questions as you think about praying kingdom prayers:

+ What are the spiritual needs? What is the big picture? How do I seek first God's kingdom in this situation?
+ What is God's vision for the situation or the person? What needs are most important? What changes might he want to make in this person?
+ What is God's will? (We discover God's will in his Word. Pray scriptures that focus on character traits that grow in trials, such as perseverance and faith.)[84]

If you are like me, you may be inundated with prayer requests. In the past I had a lot of guilt when I didn't pray daily for every request. Eventually, I learned ways of praying that eliminated my self-imposed guilt. These guidelines for intercession help me:

Pray immediately. When a woman approaches me or e-mails me with a prayer request, I no longer promise to pray later because I am prone to forget (the source of much of my guilt). Instead, I stop and pray then and there, in front of my computer or with her, whether in the midst of a crowd or over the phone.

Pray faithfully but not legalistically. Because I pray immediately, I then leave it to God to bring the person to mind as often as he wants me to pray for her. I ask the Holy Spirit to intercede according to God's will if I am uncertain how to pray (Rom. 8:26-27).

Pray in community. If a woman in need is in a group that I lead, whether it is a leadership team or a small group, there are benefits to praying together rather than simply talking about requests. It bonds the women, gives needed support and acceptance, models prayer, and builds faith. As influencers, we help others learn to pray through our examples. Many women will balk when you stop talking about their problems and replace conversation with actual prayer time, but you are leading them to the Good Shepherd who alone can meet their needs. By doing so, you influence them to recognize God as the ultimate healer and provider.

As women who desire to influence others, we must listen for the cries of others—those who are lost, scattered, injured, or sick. They need our help, and we must respond in love. Your Personal Action Plan will help you consider how to provide needed help for those whom you lead.

Personal Action Plan

Chapter 6: Baa! Baa!

Assessment

Many passages of Scripture reference shepherding. From them we can observe both good and bad shepherds. Choose at least one passage below and write down your insights into the art of shepherding. How you are doing in comparison?

John 10:1-16 (Note that the sheep also know the shepherd, who is open and vulnerable.)

Ezekiel 34:1-16

Psalm 23

Prayerfully consider each of the following statements. Think about people whom you influence, perhaps a small group, a friend, a relative, a co-worker, or children. If there is a group that you lead, use it as you think through this. Note your strengths with an **S** and your weakest areas with a **W**. Consider the shepherding passages above in addition to what you glean from the chapter.

_____ I act to know them intimately so that I know their needs and hurts.

_____ I accept each person on the same level.

_____ I am trustworthy; they know I will do as I say, keep their stories in confidence, and not gossip about them, even in the form of prayer requests.

_____ I show them that I want what is best for them.

_____ I am motivated in what I do for them out of God's love, not to get a return or out of duty.

_____ I show care for those who are hurting.

_____ I seek those who are falling away (whatever that means in your context) and encourage and challenge them.

_____ I sacrifice time and material things to care for my sheep when necessary.

_____ I invite each one to be part of our collective work together in some way.

_____ I guide them to the Good Shepherd to meet their needs rather than try to fix them myself.

_____ I support them as people even when I don't like their choices.

_____ I protect the least of these from hurt within the community I lead.

_____ I listen to them more than I talk about myself.

_____ I take the time to pray kingdom prayers for each one.

Challenge

Ask God to give you guidance and wisdom as to which of the items marked with a W need your attention most. Write them down as weaknesses below. Indicate exactly what you will do to grow in those areas listed by writing down specific goals and plans. If it is possible to implement them this week, begin today. (There is no specific number to list. Use other paper if needed and ignore the ones below if not needed.)

Weakness:

What I will do to grow:

Weakness:

What I will do to grow:

Weakness:

What I will do to grow:

Kingdom prayers

Consider each person in the group you are influencing. (If you don't have a group, think of an individual.) What is her particular situation? What kingdom prayer can you pray that fits her life right now? What is God's vision for her in the midst of her current situation according to his word? List each name and the prayer you are praying. You may prefer to write these down in your prayer journal or begin an ongoing document for this purpose.

Support

As always, you will not grow in care without support.

Whom will you ask to hold you accountable? Is there someone within the group you lead who will see how you interact with the group/individuals and really let you know how you are doing? Is there someone to whom you are already accountable—someone over you in the organizational structure? If so, talk with her about your plans for strengthening your care. Ask her to pray for you as you implement that plan. God alone can give us the love we need for the sheep.

Summary of my Plan:

My challenge(s):

Where I will get accountability and support:

CHAPTER 7

THE MIND'S EYE
COMMUNICATING VISION

> If people can't see what God is doing, they stumble all over
> themselves;
> But when they attend to what he reveals, they are most
> blessed.
>
> Proverbs 29:18, MSG

I am awed by creativity and would love to be gifted in that area. I marvel
at writers like C.S. Lewis, J.R.R. Tolkien, and J.K. Rowling who fabricate
entirely new worlds in their works of fiction. My awe at the ability of the
contestants to design unique and beautiful fashions keeps me watching
Project Runway year after year. Friends who take mundane household items
and put them together to decorate a room or table inspire me. The breadth
and variety in God's amazing world cause me to bow in wonder at the power
and design of the Creator.

In order to create something new, bringing something that doesn't yet
exist into being, we must see it first in our own mind's eye, just as all creative
people do. We must visualize it to make it reality.

Several years ago I redecorated my living area with help from my friend
Mona Crider, a professional. We decided to paint the stained paneling
and chose some lovely furniture from fabric swatches. My husband said
the samples looked great; however, when we put it all together, he hated
it. Because he failed to see it in his mind's eye, he was clueless as to how it
would look.

Building something, whether it is tangible or intangible, requires
someone to visualize in her mind's eye and clearly communicate it to those

who will implement it. The very nature of leadership is mobilizing others to fulfill a vision, which only happens when the dream is caught in a way that people make it their own. Communicating vision is the fifth fundamental of leadership. It is what separates leaders from followers. Communicating God's vision to someone else who embraces that dream makes you a spiritual leader.

What is Vision?

> Vision is a picture of the future that produces passion in people.[85]
>
> Bill Hybels

Vision is a God-given picture of a possible future for a person or group, accompanied by a God-given burden to see it accomplished. Pastor Andy Stanley says it well: "Vision is a clear mental picture of what could be, fueled by the conviction that it should be."[86]

Vision is what gets a leader excited and motivates her to keep going. It is her dreams for a better tomorrow, as God gives them to her. Bill Hybels, founder of Willow Creek Community Church and leadership expert, describes it as "the most potent weapon for world change."[87]

Vision sees missionary organizations where there are none. Vision pictures churches providing food for the poor and clinics for the ill. Vision imagines ways to bring justice to victims. Vision plants churches. Vision sees a friend's life transformed by God. Vision finds ways to reach out to neighbors in love. When vision becomes reality, the world is indeed changed.

Vision vs. Mission

Previously we considered the leadership fundamental we identified as personal calling. We noted that each of us has a unique mission at the intersection of design, burden, and opportunity. That life purpose works in tandem with a God-given vision that focuses on results. As you follow your calling, what you see in your mind's eye as a possible outcome is your vision. Although your mission never changes, the dream may. In fact, a leader may realize several visions during her life.

Late Christian education expert Kenneth Gangel explains the difference between vision and mission:

Mission is that simple and terse statement that identifies why an organization exists and what it expects to do on earth. Vision then describes how that organization will design its future to achieve its mission. Vision grows out of mission, but they are hardly identical concepts. In one important way, however, vision and mission are alike—they are both unique to the individual organization.[88]

I would amend his statement to include individuals. You have a mission and your vision will design your future to accomplish it.

Years ago, our women's ministry at Northwest Bible Church developed this mission statement:

> Northwest Bible Church's Women's Ministry exists to
> CONNECT women
>   To Christ
>   To women of other ages and stages
>   To ministry service
> So that we grow together in the faith and love of Jesus Christ.

Vision gave legs to these purposes by revealing how to accomplish this mission. Vision sought women disconnected from Jesus and pictured them coming to the yearly Christmas luncheon where they heard and responded to the gospel. Vision saw groups of women of all ages interacting in Women's Connection Groups and small groups. Vision planned leadership classes to connect women to areas of service that matched their gifts. We could have done things a hundred different ways to fulfill that mission. But these are things that God laid on our hearts.

Receiving God's Vision

For spiritual leadership, vision must come from God. We must be sure that we are pursuing God's vision for his people rather than our own. His plan will align with his work in the world at large, building his kingdom in his people through the church.

The first thing that leads to vision is a burden. We noted that burden is one identifier that leads us to our life purposes. Well, it leads to vision as well, which makes sense because the vision should line up with its mission.

When God wants to change things, he puts a problem on a person's heart so that she will seek a solution.

Bill Hybels calls it "holy discontent." He says in his book on the subject, "What wrecks the heart of someone who loves God is often the *very thing* God wants to use to fire them up to do something that, under normal circumstances, they would never attempt to do."[89] That burden leads to a dream of what should be, the picture of God's solution.

A vision is an answer to a problem. How do we fix it? What must we do to change things?

One of the most detailed stories of vision comes from the Old Testament. Nehemiah lived in the days when the Jews were exiled from their land. In God's sovereign timing and plan, Nehemiah became the cupbearer for the Persian King Artaxerxes I. Because of his position at the royal court, Nehemiah had access to the powerful king who ruled his ancestors' land of Israel.

Nehemiah received God's vision for Jerusalem, providing us a great example to study. I suggest that you read Nehemiah 1:1-2:8 to follow the story.

First, Nehemiah's vision was born out of a burden that arose from a conversation with some men from Jerusalem. He learned from them that the city walls were in disrepair and its gates destroyed, making the inhabitants prey to their enemies. Nehemiah's responses reveal the depth of his burden:

- Mourning and crying (1:4)
- Fasting and praying (1:4)
- Solitude (1:4)
- Confession (1:6-9)
- Petitioning God to fulfill the vision based on his promises (1:9-11)
- Waiting on God's timing (4 months between 1:1 and 2:1)

Rather than proceed on impulse, Nehemiah took time alone to petition God and ask him to move on behalf of his people. He waited for God's vision of what was to be. Then, when the opportunity to act presented itself, Nehemiah took advantage of it.

Bill Hybels shares further thoughts about receiving God's vision. He highlights the importance of the right attitudes for listening to him:

- Yielded to God

- ✦ Truly desiring his vision, not his blessing on yours
- ✦ Rid of distractions
- ✦ Read, heard, seen, visited—gotten out of your box[90]

Note how many tips for finding God's vision flow out of the first two leadership fundamentals: centered on Christ and character. Every other spiritual leadership fundamental depends on those two essentials being in place.

Hybels's last point is very important: leaders read, research, and talk to people outside of their normal Christian culture. They aren't afraid to listen to others. They aren't too proud to believe that someone else may have a good idea; in fact, it may be even better.

When leaders begin borrowing too much from others, however, they may be taking shortcuts to listening to God who deals with people, churches, and situations individually. Often what works somewhere else may not succeed in a different context. That is why Christian researcher George Barna says that recognizing God's vision depends upon knowing your context.[91]

I find it helpful to gather lots of thoughts and ideas and let God take those and make something new out of them. God in his wisdom forces us to seek him for the unique vision for each context. God wants us to depend upon him rather than borrow answers from others. When I realized that Heart-to-Heart, the amazing mentoring program begun by Vickie Kraft,[92] was floundering at our church, I knew that we had an issue. What was God's vision to continue prioritizing relationships between older and younger women? As we prayed and listened to women and considered the causes of the problem, my leadership team and I envisioned groups of women united around various activities that they enjoyed in common. As a result, we developed Women's Connection Groups to supply opportunities for women to interact among the generations.

I previously shared my personal mission statement with you: my mission is to teach God's Word, to train godly leaders, and to give vision and simplicity to ministry so that others are challenged to grow as vessels for God's use in the world. For years as a volunteer leader in my church, I was burdened about the lack of leadership development. I had received some excellent training through Precept Ministries. Why did I have to go outside of my church to be equipped? Why wasn't the church doing it? After all, scripture requires it:

> It was he who gave some as apostles, some as prophets, some as evangelists, and some as pastors and teachers, to equip the saints for the work of ministry, that is, to build up the body of Christ, until we all attain to the unity of the faith and of the knowledge of the Son of God—a mature person, attaining to the measure of Christ's full stature (Ephesians 4:11-13).

Although I had a God-given vision to develop leaders, I did nothing about it; yet over time I dreamed about what I would do if I could. When I did my seminary internship, I recognized it as my opportunity and asked if I could develop a leadership training class for women. It was God's time and I had a plan. I just had to communicate the vision to my internship mentor and to a highly placed female leader who could help me fulfill the vision by doing some of the teaching.

Since then, I have taught and revised the information on spiritual leadership a number of times. God used further reading and my own experiences as a leader to improve and develop the training from that original class. I didn't rush in and try to convince others of my good idea, but I waited and watched for God to bring about the right situation where I was being invited to implement something new. I was ready to communicate God's vision when the time came.

Communicating God's Vision

> Painting a verbal picture is the essence of visioncasting.[93]
> Andy Stanley

Unless others catch the vision, we aren't leading them and the dream will never be realized. The essence of leadership involves influencing others to buy into the leader's vision and work toward accomplishing it. I have read a number of books on leadership in the business world, and every author emphasized the necessity of communicating often and well why we do what we do. Casting vision well means that others catch it.

Over the years I have envisioned solutions as I encountered problems and new situations. Some of those became practical plans for ministry while others required time and opportunities that never arose. I could see how to structure and accomplish the vision, but I had to get others to visualize the dream for themselves in order to bring it to life. Unless we communicate our ideas well, there will be little buy-in by others.

Let's continue Nehemiah's story by reading Nehemiah 2:3-5, 11-18, to see how he cast vision:

- He painted a picture of the problem (2:3, 17).
- He pictured the solution (2:3, 17).
- He gave the "why," explaining the reason it must be done (2:17).
- He testified of God's work behind the scenes so far, which reinforces the "why" (2:18).
- He called others to immediate action, helping them see "why now" (2:18).[94]

God was on the move and gave Nehemiah a burden and a vision, and Nehemiah followed. He acted when presented with the opportunity, and he led others to recognize what God was calling the community to do.

The way we cast vision is vitally important. We must pass our own burden to others and help them picture the solution in their own mind's eye. For them to see what we see, we must confidently and enthusiastically share the vision with clarity and simplicity. If we impart too many details or seem blasé ourselves, we will be unable to motivate anyone else to accomplish the dream.

Hybels speaks with honesty, "Sometimes whole visions live or die on the basis of the words the leader chooses for articulating that vision."[95]

Stanley has some practical pointers for communicating dreams:

- State the vision simply.
- Cast the vision convincingly.
- Repeat the vision regularly.
- Celebrate the vision systematically.
- Embrace the vision personally.[96]

Our words matter. Good leaders spend time finding the clear, simple words to communicate their visions. If we don't take the time to confirm God's vision, we can never have the confidence to enlist others well. A leader calls others to participate and does so clearly enough that they respond.

My friend Katie experienced a difficult divorce, which left her money tied up in retirement accounts. Although she owned the house, she had little disposable income because of her low-paying job. I grieved over her situation and prayed for her, asking God to give her wisdom. One day when we talked about her struggles, I was able to share a vision of the problem and solution in a way that she could visualize it. I verbally painted a portrait of her looking longingly out of her house, which had bars over the windows and doors. Although her house imprisoned her, Katie had the key to freedom by leaving it. Although she was unable to make that decision in the midst of a very hard time, I planted a vision and left it to God to bring it to life.

Women who See the Unseen

> Now faith is being sure of what we hope for, being convinced of what we do not see.
>
> Hebrews 11:1

I love it when people believe that God is at work to draw others to Jesus. Jody Curran deliberately reaches out to her neighbors, hoping and praying to attract them to him. When I asked her how she casts vision of a life of faith, this was her answer:

> I think the best way to communicate that vision is by living out your faith and sharing what God is doing in your life when you can. Loving people is not hard if you remember that God loves you and he did even in the worst parts of your life. Friends and family have modeled for me how easy it is to be intentional in your interactions with people— being gracious and kind to the people around you—in your everyday travels and especially with neighbors.[97]

Because she doesn't know the details of her neighbors' lives, she casts vision of life with Jesus through her own experience: "I only know what he did in my life and I recommend him on that basis."[98]

Think about specific situations in which you find yourself right now. Consider people and their problems as well as situations that present difficulties. What holy discontent may be involved? What vision would fix it? Do you lead a small group? What do you visualize for them? Do you have children? What is God's vision for their lives? What does God want to see happen in your community? In people's hearts? In homes near you? What needs to change and how can you with your gifting and burdens accomplish it with others?

Mary DeMuth writes fiction to lead women who deal with the hurts of the past to spiritual health: "I love to paint a picture for my readers to see what life would be like if they would choose to pursue healing from the past. I don't paint it rosy; I do share the realities of how hard it is to heal, how brave one must be. I do share that it's definitely worth the effort. You never grow and change if you don't dare to open up the wounds of the past."[99]

My long-time friend Patsy Bolin has three young grandsons, and her goal is that they walk with God. I asked her how she moves them toward that vision. She has so many ways to show them Christ that she needs to write her own book for grandparents. Basically, she models a life of following Jesus through her words, her actions, and her teaching. She spends time creatively showing them who God is and what he desires for each of them. Her own relationship with God is a living vision of what she wants theirs to be. I know that it's easy to love and care for our children and grandchildren, but Patsy deliberately sets out to help them visualize what it means to follow Christ. She works to influence them spiritually. Now that I have grandchildren, I hope Patsy writes that book.[100]

Your own Buy In—Walk the Talk

You can't lead others where you haven't gone yourself. Patsy and Mary both model their words for those whom they influence. To be a spiritual leader, you must be growing spiritually. To lead others to catch vision, you must so believe in it yourself that others trust you. When they see that you sacrifice for the dream and act to bring it to pass, they recognize that it is possible and real. If a leader casts vision in any way that makes it iffy, others will wait and see before committing themselves. As Hybels says, "Leaders have to own it."[101]

I laugh and tell people that my husband and I have built churches all over Texas, and it's close to the truth. We have given money for recreation buildings, chapels, worship centers, and educational space in five different churches in our state, not including memorial gifts to the building funds of other churches. I have seen building campaigns that failed and others that produced more money than the goal. There is one essential key in raising needed funds for such plans—buy-in. If the church leadership doesn't fully believe that God is in the vision, if they give any hints that it's a wait and see idea, or if they don't ask unashamedly and enthusiastically for the money, it is doomed.

When you have a vision to cast, ask yourself these questions:

+ What have I sacrificed for the vision that shows I am 100% invested in its fulfillment?
+ What actions am I taking to bring the vision to pass?

If you have to think too hard, you haven't owned the vision and it likely will not succeed.

Reinforce the Vision

All good parents know that they must reinforce the behavior they want in their children or the kids will revert to their old habits. As the visionary, you must find ways to do that with the dream. Consider these examples:

+ If you envision your child as an independent adult, how do you reinforce that as you go? What behaviors do you reward? How do you reward them?
+ How often do you talk about the vision with those you hope to influence and find markers of success to celebrate small or large steps toward fulfilling the vision?
+ What are some ways to "pay" volunteers? What reinforcement has worked for you when you have been volunteering somewhere?

When we reinforce behavior that moves the vision forward, we also have opportunity to remind everyone involved what the dream looks like. Hybels declares that vision leaks.[102] If we don't continue to pour it into the minds of our followers, they lose it. When ministry or life gets hard, people abandon the dream unless someone continues to re-paint the vision. Stanley explains why: "Vision is about what *could* be and what *should* be, but my life is about *right this minute*."[103]

As I write this book, I have encountered so many obstacles. Without the encouragement of my husband and good friends who remind me to stick to the dream, I would have abandoned it long ago. We all need reinforcement from time to time, even the leader.

Pray about the vision, believing that God will bring to maturity the dream that he birthed.

If you see God's vision for yourself, a ministry, your children, your friends, your small group, or anyone else whom you influence, in the end you must give it to God. You cannot realize a dream until the timing is right for others to catch it. Until then, wait on God, entrusting the problem and solution to him.

Think Moses! His initial attempts to free his people from Egyptian slavery were unsuccessful; in fact, they resulted in additional grief (Exodus 5-6). God's own people weren't on board with his plans and refused to believe Moses when he shared the vision. Moses' response was to continue asking Pharaoh for permission to leave while giving the answer to God. You likely know the rest of the story.

Use your waiting time to allow God to tweak the dream until it is entirely his. Your job is to faithfully cast the vision until others respond.

My hope is that you will begin to discover a dream for those whom you already influence. How can you cast a vision that will motivate change? It may be a dream you already have but have never put into a simple and clear statement. It may be a vision that you have held but failed to communicate to them. There are likely situations and problems that you will face this very week that need vision-casting. Be aware of them and speak with clarity and enthusiasm, and you never know how God will use you.

If you have never previously considered vision, you can't expect to receive it from God in a day. But begin seeking it now and watch God give you a burden and a vision of the solution. Then, cast it and begin the work God prepared for you in eternity past.

Personal Action Plan

Chapter 7: The Mind's Eye

Assessment

Defining the vision

Assess where you are with a vision for a group or individual whom you currently lead or influence.

Describe a situation right now where you are or can be an influencer (leader) of others. Describe the people whom you have an opportunity to influence.

Do you currently have a vision for them? If so, what is it? If not, what bothers you about them or the situation? Has God given you a holy burden about something that needs to change that fits into his kingdom agenda? If so, describe it.

Communicating the vision

Assess yourself in a previous attempt to move others toward a dream. If you wrote down a vision in the previous section, consider how you have attempted to pass it on. If not, think through a time when you wanted something to happen in another person's life or in your world at large. How did you communicate that to get others to embrace it? Did you share the four elements needed in good vision casting: the problem, the solution, the reason it must be done, and the reason it must be done now?

Rate your attempts from 1-4, with 4 meaning fully achieved.

_____ Clarity of your communication
_____ Simplicity of your communication
_____ Repetition of your communication
_____ Motivation in your communication
_____ Illustrations in your communication
_____ Your own 100% buy-in to the vision
_____ Your sacrifices to make the vision happen
_____ Your reinforcement of others' positive actions toward vision
_____ Your prayer time for the vision

Challenge

Defining God's vision

Your first challenge is to see God's vision where you are currently leading. Spend time in prayer for the people whom you presently influence. Ask God to give you his burden for a problem with individuals or the group and show you a solution. You may need to spend several days or even weeks on this. Think about scriptures that might apply. Keep seeking God and listening to him. He may use his Word, a circumstance, or another person to burden your heart with a vision of change, or he may simply speak to you in solitude and silence. God's vision will correlate with his work in the world so be sure they align.

Write down the thoughts that you have so far. It doesn't have to be a grand vision, so don't get caught up in looking for something outside of your influence. Perhaps you lead a small group; if so, your vision for that group may be about more intimacy in sharing or about more faithfulness in prayer as a group. Your sphere of influence may be at home right now; if so, your vision may be that your children will seek God for their decisions. You may see another problem that burdens you. What vision do you have for changing the situation? What end result can you see for the one(s) you have in mind? Picture a preferred future, and write down what you envision. This may be the same vision you have always had. If so, you are way ahead!

Communicating the vision

Consider the dream that God is laying on your heart. In light of your assessment, begin to work toward communicating it well.

Write down the four aspects of good communication as they relate to your vision:

The problem

The solution

The reason it must be done

The reason it must be done now

How can you make the vision clear in your communication? Brainstorm simple, clear verbiage.

What stories or illustrations will you use to motivate others to embrace the vision?

What actions will you take so that others know that you are 100% invested in the vision and are working toward making it happen yourself?

What positive actions in others will you reinforce? How will you reinforce them?

How will you continually recast the vision so that it sticks?

Support

As always, you will not grow much in this fundamental without support. Think about how to get support in the following areas and write down your plan.

What person would give great input as you share your ideas for stating the vision clearly and simply? (Make sure it's someone who will be honest and perhaps help you brainstorm.)

What person might have ideas about ways you can reinforce behavior that positively moves the group toward the vision? Contact her.

Summary of my Plan:

My challenge(s):

My support in reaching this challenge:

CHAPTER 8

HAVING THE KNOW-HOW
COMPETENCE

> Competence goes beyond words. It's the leader's ability to
> say it, plan it, and do it in such a way that others know that
> you know how—and know that they want to follow you.[104]
>
> John Maxwell

Recently, the faucets to the sink in our utility room and the tub in our
bathroom began to drip. (I think the manufacturers design them to go out
after a certain number of years so they break at the same time.) Although our
plumber took care of the problem at the sink easily, he had to temporarily
stop the water to the tub from dripping while he searched for the right
parts. Just after he left, I turned on the tub water to check his work, but it
came out brown. When I shut it off, the dripping began again; in fact, it
became a steady but slow stream rather than merely a trickle. My husband
declared that he could fix it and made a quick trip to the garage for some
tools. Within minutes of his attempted repair job, the water was violently
gushing out and splashing all over the bathroom. When his valiant efforts
were unsuccessful, he turned off the connection to the house and called the
plumber to return. Thankfully, the professional was able to stop the flow
inside until he could return with the needed parts.

My husband would be the first to admit that he needs to stay away
from complicated plumbing issues. Although he does a great job with small
repairs, he doesn't have the know-how to fix big problems. It's best to either
leave such issues to those who have the skills or go to a class to learn to
repair plumbing the right way. Sometimes we just need to know that we
don't know.

Two Levels of Competence

The final fundamental of leadership is competence, which is necessary to a leader on two levels. First, leading others requires the leadership know-how to harness their abilities. Secondly, the leader must be knowledgeable enough about the overall goal and the various tasks required of her team to see that they are accomplished. Basically, she must have competence in leadership and the know-how required for the job.

Are these two levels of competence also necessary when exerting influence over an individual? Certainly! A mother must exhibit good parenting skills to maximize her influence over her children (the leadership know-how) as well as help them increasingly develop the abilities they need for life (the know-how for her followers). If a parent's goal is to raise strong, independent, and godly children, she must set that vision before them and give them opportunities to develop their own competence, which involves teaching them needed skills. Mentors must have abilities on two levels as well: competence in the knowledge and skill being passed on to their mentees and the leadership know-how to maximize their influence.

When we think of leadership, the typical image of a team leader or small group leader may come to mind. Again, I think of D'Ann, who as chair of a luncheon committee must understand the tasks involved in putting on a large event as well as know how to guide a team to work together. I am also reminded of Val, who coaches small group leaders. To mentor the women whom she trains to facilitate and lead small groups, she needs knowledge and experience in directing such groups herself. In addition, she must have the ability to cast vision so that the leaders visualize what a small group can become.

Are there leadership skills other than the fundamentals we have discussed in the previous chapters that are important to leadership? Absolutely! The necessary know-how depends on the vision and the position. As you approach a leadership role, carefully assess the skills that may be involved.

My experience taught me that leading women's ministries requires, among other skills, developing a team and recruiting and organizing volunteers. The position also involves the ability to strategically plan and implement a ministry vision. Almost any leadership role that involves dealing with groups of people requires the know-how to effect change and manage conflict, and my positions did also. My latest job description included writing Bible study curriculum and large group Bible teaching, as well as developing small groups. Not every woman who leads a ministry needs the same skills, but they were important competencies for my position.

If you want to be successful, it is imperative that you become aware of what you must know and do in your role of influence.

Discovering what Know-How is Needed

What specific abilities do you need to be a competent leader? What knowledge should you have? What practical skills should you develop? Each position has its own set of requirements.

When I was a church volunteer, I had no clue about skills I might need. Someone asked me to serve, and I agreed. Every time I began a new role, it seemed that I quickly realized that I needed help. Although I knew there was likely a beneficial book out there somewhere, I was at a loss as to what book would help—or even what skill was needed.

Here are some of the specific skills and knowledge I needed as a ministry leader. Maybe my list will help you discover areas where you need competence, even if you lead one individual.

Skills:
+ Writing a mission statement
+ Recruiting a team
+ Structuring a team or committee
+ Building a team mentality
+ Dealing with conflict
+ Writing job descriptions
+ Leading a meeting
+ Preparing an agenda
+ Setting deadlines for team members by developing a timeline
+ Dealing with ineffective team members
+ Implementing change
+ Budgeting or following a budget
+ Prioritizing time and resources

Knowledge:
+ Understanding the group's goals
+ Recognizing the role and tasks of each team member
+ Understanding the limits of my authority, i.e., what must be approved and/or delegated elsewhere

Was I competent in all these areas when I first accepted this kind of position? No! However, I had experience with most of them and worked hard to grow in the others. In time, God graciously sent me wise individuals who could give me counsel and help, as well as speak truth into my leadership. If I had not been open to suggestions, other people may have quit following me pretty quickly.

What skills and knowledge do you need if you are attempting to influence a friend spiritually? You must know how to pray for her, to lead her to faith, to refer her to pertinent verses, and to encourage her with stories from your own experience with God. You need the ability to ask good questions about her and her life so that you can learn to love her well. (*Chapter 6: Baa! Baa! Care* can help you gain skills in this area.)

Jot down competencies that come to your mind that would help you carry out your present role of influence.

One way to discover the skills and knowledge necessary to your leadership is to ask someone who has experience. Who had the job before you? What friends or acquaintances have experience in similar roles? Once you identify what you need to know and do to lead well where you are, your next task is to find ways to acquire the know-how that you lack.

Getting the Needed Know-How

Assessing our own abilities in tasks such as chairing a meeting, leading a small group, or recruiting volunteers may require an objective outsider. Where can you find such help? A mentor or coach, someone with experience who can observe and give feedback, is invaluable. The right person can guide you to ways of acquiring expertise. She may suggest books or classes, or it may be that her wisdom and experience will provide you with all that you need to know.

What is the difference between a mentor and a coach? It is said that a mentor gives out the answers while a coach helps others discover for themselves what works, but I don't see that difference in real life. If an answer is needed, both give it. If training is helpful, both make suggestions. Both good mentors and coaches observe their mentees and give suggestions for improvement. Both share their own experience and expertise as needed. So call it any term you prefer, but find someone with the skills and knowledge to help you grow in your proficiency.

Few of us will enjoy the kind of learning experience enjoyed by the twelve disciples. They traveled and lived with Jesus, experiencing the most intense personal attention possible. In such a case, the mentee initially learns from his mentor; then he tries it and receives feedback; finally, he is on his own (see Luke 9:1-10; 10:1-24). The mentor gives his disciples his time and friendship first and foremost, and they learn from his example. Mark tells us that Jesus "appointed twelve, that they might be with Him, and that He might send them out to preach, and to have authority to cast out the demons" (Mark 3:14-15, NASB). The twelve disciples were first "with him," able to watch and hear Jesus, ask him questions, and learn firsthand from the Master.

Such opportunities are rare in our culture, but the more we are able to simply spend time with those who have been where we are, the better we grow. I never had an official mentor or the kind of experience that the disciples enjoyed, but I used every opportunity I had to learn what I needed to know.

Most of my leadership know-how came from my involvement with Precept Ministries.[105] Although I taught a Bible study in my church for several years, I had received no training. I did my best, but it was frustrating. When I attended my first workshop to qualify to use Precept curriculum, I gained valuable skills in studying the Bible and leading a group discussion. Over the next few years, I gravitated toward the many levels and types of training offered, even repeating some workshops so that I could get the maximum benefit. I learned how to observe, interpret, and apply the Bible, and I also watched godly women who mentored me without knowing it. Kay Arthur, the founder of the ministry and its primary teacher, modeled the passion that a teacher should have for God, his Word, and his people. Her knowledge of the Scripture inspired me to teach thoroughly and well. Other staff members equipped me to train other leaders, passing on the skills they taught me. Each of them affected me in a different way, and I remain grateful for the influence they had in my life.

Although I gained much from the Precept staff, my need for increased competence as a Bible teacher led me to Dallas Seminary. In addition to knowledge of God's Word, my professors taught me some practical skills, such as discovering and implementing vision. When I joined a cohort of like-minded women for my Doctor of Ministry degree at Gordon-Conwell Theological Seminary, I had the privilege of sitting under Dr. Alice Mathews over the course of three years. Her heart for women and her knowledge of ministry to them helped me grow in competence as a leader of women. Her personal integrity and care for us made a difference for all of us in our class, and I know that my care of others improved from her example.

As my experience proves, we often need the influence of a number of people to help us develop competence. You may ask an older woman for parenting advice or look to an experienced leader to help you improve in facilitating a small group. A great administrator's suggestions for how to organize volunteers may be invaluable while her help in planning a meeting agenda is weak. Find someone who isn't afraid to challenge you with truth and will support you when you stumble.

You may be reluctant to take the initiative to find a coach. It is highly unlikely, however, that anyone will offer to mentor you otherwise. You might begin by inviting a possible candidate to meet you for coffee or lunch. See how well you relate, and ask her questions about her own experience. If your interaction is valuable and you see in her the type of leader you want to become, ask her for ongoing help without using the term "mentor." (It's a scary word because it suggests a level of expertise that few of us think we have.) Just ask her to observe you and give suggestions or to meet with you periodically for input.

Claudia McGuire, who serves as Leadership Coaching Pastor at Chase Oaks Church, intentionally found help in her staff role:

> In the past couple of years . . . it began to dawn on me that I really don't develop anyone. I can plan programs or workshops to help people learn and develop their skills, but I can't develop them. As a coach once told me; "I can teach them, but I can't learn them."[106]

> I became frustrated in this new role. That led me to check out a life coach. For the past year, through this life coach, I have been learning so much about myself, my communication style, and how I do ministry. In other words, after being extremely outwardly focused for too long, I needed to take a fresh look at myself, spend some time listening to God, and make some changes, which I'm still working on.

> The beauty of a life coach is that we have phone conversations, so our discussions are easily scheduled on my calendar. I

have homework assignments. She asks me tough questions. I have accountability. Progress is measured. And she makes me think like no other. I love that![107]

Claudia sought out someone to help her develop her leadership competence, and that often involves a hard look within. Such mentors or coaches can be invaluable when we are willing to listen to their input and spend time with God to discover areas of needed change.

As you grow as a leader, provide the same benefit for those who follow you. Look for women who are ready to learn, and invest your friendship and time in them. The best leaders are always looking for their replacements and passing on their know-how.

Take time to assess yourself. If you are struggling in your leadership, determine if you are misplaced in a position where you are not gifted or whether you simply need to work at becoming competent. Don't keep trying to do something for which you aren't equipped, or you may bring disaster upon yourself and your followers, as my non-plumber husband nearly did.

The responsibility to grow the know-how is yours alone. Use the Personal Action Plan to help you work through this material. Invite a woman to give you input into your leadership, and expect God to use her in more ways than you initially anticipate. My guess is that you will make a lifelong friend in the process and that your friendship will bless her in return.

Personal Action Plan

Chapter 8: Having the Know-How

Assessment

Defining places of influence
In what situation(s) do you want to increase your influence on others? What specific people or groups do you want to spiritually influence? (Ideally, we want our faith to be a light to others in more than one setting.)

Defining competencies
You may want to think about this part of the assessment over several days so that you have time to mull over your answer. Considering only the areas of influence that you wrote down above, what skills and knowledge do you need in order to create a high level of competence just doing the job that is required in that field? (At this point don't consider leadership skills or essentials.)

For example, here are some competencies I needed, not to be a leader of women but just to do my job:

- Skills: Writing a Bible lesson; teaching the Bible; recruiting volunteers, dealing with conflict
- Knowledge: Theological and biblical understanding; peacemaking principles

Now it's your turn. Write down the abilities that you need in your area(s). You may want to divide yours into skills and knowledge as well. If you are a parent, what do you need to know and do? What know-how do you need in your workplace? Your community position?

Review your list. Mark competencies where you are weak with a **W**. Indicate strengths with an **S**.

Now consider what leadership skills (not our fundamentals) you need in order to lead others in the areas of your influence. (You may want to review the list of skills and knowledge I gave in the chapter to get you started thinking.) Mark them in the same way as in the previous list.

Finally, prayerfully consider the following leadership fundamentals we have covered that require competency and mark them as you did the others:

Communicating vision

Care

Challenge

The know-how for your specific area

Take the first list you made and individually consider those which you marked as weak. What can you do to improve your abilities? Write down anything that comes to mind that may help you grow. Then mark the ideas which you will definitely implement; choose at least one. For example, will you get a mentor to help you? Will you attend a conference, take a class, read some books on the subject? Will you observe another leader in the same field?

The know-how for leadership

Considering the second and third lists of competencies related to your leadership that are marked with a W, which one or two is God most encouraging you to work on right now? Write down anything that comes to mind to help you improve your proficiency in those areas. Then, mark the ideas you will definitely do.

Support

Mentors/coaches
It is likely time to seriously consider befriending someone who has competence in areas where you are weak. You may be able to think of one particular mentor who is accomplished in every skill, or you may need several different coaches.

First, write down the qualities you want in a mentor. Spiritual mentors should exhibit some of the characteristics we have covered, such as centered in Christ and character. The best coaches speak the truth in love to their mentees. Although it may be painful to hear, the best leaders are open to change and want others to help them see themselves as they are. Second, write down the skills that you want her to teach you.

Now brainstorm names of women who fit your criteria. Pray about the list and prioritize the names in each area of growth.

Supportive people
Now, think about other support that you need as you continue growing as a leader for the rest of your life. You need prayer support, encouragement, and wise advice. Prayerfully consider people who will hold you accountable, pray for you, and give you wise words as needed. You may want peers or those with more experience than you have. They may never meet together or you may desire them to meet with you as a group, almost like your personal board of directors or advisors.

Brainstorm possibilities and write down the qualities each person would provide.

Summary of my Plan:
I will challenge myself in these competencies in these ways:

1. _____
2. _____
3. _____

I will approach the following people about supporting me in the next _____ weeks

- To help grow me in competence as a leader

- To help me grow in the know-how of my job or that of my followers

- To give me support through prayer, encouragement, and wisdom

CONCLUSION

MOVING BEYOND ORDINARY

Sue Edward's Story

My story focuses on the women who saved my life—really. Are you thinking I'm one of those women who go to extremes to create a compelling story? In this case, I'm not overstating what happened. Some women really did save my life.

I was a mess. My mother's problems spilled over into my life and by the time I married at 24, I was hyper-emotional, unable to make decisions, and often severely depressed. I loved my husband but did not know how to express that love well, and he didn't know how either. We dreamed of a big family and God gave us two little girls in the first two years of our union. An only child myself, I had no clue how to parent. As a result, I was exhausted and angry. As my husband withdrew from my dysfunction, I spiraled down even more, plagued by suicidal thoughts.

Then my neighbor invited me to a women's Bible study. My grandmother was the only authentic Christian I had ever known, but she died when I was eight. She bequeathed me her Bible. So I tied my long stringy hair into a pony tail, tucked that Bible under my arm, and joined my friend for my first Bible study. The women gathered first in small groups, where they dug into the scriptures and shared their lives with each other, even the gnarly stuff. They were real. They were fun. And, wonder of wonders, they liked me. After the group time, a lovely woman taught the whole group more about the verses we studied, her voice strong and caring. She saw me. She even spoke to me afterwards.

The leader of the group called me several days after we met and thanked me for my input. The beautiful teacher lady sent me an encouraging note in the mail--the first note like that I had ever received. It's in the bottom of a big keepsake box today. Wednesday became the best day of the week. In time, these women re-mothered me, pointing me to Jesus.

Over the next fifteen years, they guided me step by step to health. They taught me how to pray, to understand the Bible, to love my husband well, to be the mother my daughters needed, and that Jesus would make up for the lack. I learned ministry skills--how to lead small groups, how to love and encourage women, how to write Bible curriculum, and finally, how to teach the Bible. I attended seminary to become a better Bible teacher for my friends there.

They loved me despite my failings. Once, they tried to push me too fast, thinking I was ready to administer one of their six Bible classes. I thought I could lead for them, but when several women leaders had to drop out of leadership, I took their resignations personally. I wasn't yet strong enough to weather the ups and downs of leadership. After my melt-down, the teacher lady stepped in for me, adding to her already too full plate. But she did not shame me and continued to believe in me. They asked me again several years later. I am forever grateful.

Today I teach in the seminary I attended earlier, as a full-time tenured professor, equipping men and women from all over the world for ministry. I have written four leadership books and nine Bible studies for women. I've trained women in Africa and Russia. My girls are grown and thriving, with families of their own. My husband and I have learned to love one another well, and he spends his discretionary time discipling men in prisons. Sometimes when I meet with women students, they think I have led a charmed life. What they don't know is that I am simply a product of a group of women who chose to love like Jesus, and with Him, they saved my life. Anybody can do it, and my passion is to simply pass it on.[108]

Sue's account of moving from ordinary woman to spiritual leader is really the story of a group of women who dared to be spiritual leaders. They reached out to her, influenced her, mentored her, and cared for her. They gave her a vision of a different life found in Christ and a call on her life to lead. What a wonderful tribute to them and a challenge to us to be just as intentional about influencing others! We never know how God will use those whom we touch for his kingdom's sake.

Your Story

Your journey of growing from ordinary woman to spiritual leader is being written today as you choose to develop in the fundamentals. God's desire is that you affect those within your sphere of influence, whether they are large groups, small groups, or individuals. He has placed you exactly where he wants you to be as salt and light to those around you. You can spread the love of Christ, touching your friends, family, co-workers, and neighbors through your life and your words by God's grace and power.

Your Personal Action Plan develops a practical strategy to become the spiritual leader you are meant to be. The end of your story is waiting to be written. You can move beyond ordinary. Go for it!

Personal Action Plan

Moving Beyond Ordinary

Assessment

Spend time reviewing the six fundamentals of leadership: centered in Christ, character, calling, care, communicating vision, and competency. You may want to read through the titles of the subsections of the chapters or review your previous personal action plans. Prayerfully spend time answering these questions:

- In which one or two of the essentials do you most need to grow in light of your current places of influence?

- What leadership fundamental will best help you increase your spiritual influence in relationships you already have?

Challenge

Review your answers to the personal action plans which follow the chapters on the essentials you noted above. What 3-5 actions can you take to continue growing in those areas?

Support

What support do you need long-term to develop those fundamentals? A mentor/coach? An accountability/prayer partner? A small group? What person or group will you approach?

Implementing a Long-term Plan
My plan to grow in areas of weakness:

My plan to get support while I work on those areas:

Put all of your Personal Action Plans in a prominent place as a reminder to periodically review them. Consider reassessing yourself and developing new challenges at least once a year. You may want to do so each January to develop goals and support for the coming year.

My ongoing plan to assess myself, challenge myself, and support myself beyond this year:

APPENDIX

SPIRITUAL GIFT CHART

Gift	Definition	Passages	Characteristics
Administration	Ability to organize & implement God's vision	1 Cor. 12:28	Organizes a task, making it simple
Apostle	Appointed to share the gospel in the name & under the authority of Christ in new area	1 Cor. 12:28, 29; Eph. 4:11	Ability & desire to go into an unreached area and bring the gospel
Discernment of spirits	Ability to discern what is of Satan and what is of God	1 Cor. 12:10	Concerned for origin of ideas, theology, programs
Performing miracles	Ability to supersede the laws of nature	1 Cor. 12:10, 28, 29	Miracles overcome the laws of nature
Exhortation	Ability to come alongside to encourage & challenge others	Rom. 12:8	Encourages or confronts graciously & people listen
Evangelist	Ability to share the gospel with clarity & power	Eph. 4:11	People respond to her presentation of Jesus
Faith	Ability to believe God for extraordinary things	1 Cor. 12:9	Trusts God to move in challenging situations
Gifts of healing	Ability to heal supernaturally	1 Cor. 12:9, 28, 30	Physical healing is seen immediately
Giving	Ability to give with joy & generosity	Rom. 12:8	Constantly gives to others & ministry; not always rich

Gift	Definition	Passages	Characteristics
Helps/service	Ability to see what needs to be done & do it	Rom. 12:7; 1 Cor. 12:28	Loves to work behind the scenes
Interpretation of tongues	Ability to interpret a language without having studied it	1 Cor. 12:10, 30	Can hear a new language and understand it
Kinds of tongues	Ability to speak in a language without having studied it	1 Cor. 12:10. 28, 30; 14:1-40	Speaks of Jesus in a language she doesn't know
Leadership	Ability to cast a vision that others follow	Rom. 12:8	Sees vision and inspires followers to achieve it
Mercy	Ability to see physical needs and meet them	Rom. 12:8	Enjoys working with sick, elderly, etc.
Pastor-teacher	Shepherds & feeds God's flock from the Word	Eph. 4:11	Loving concern for spiritual health of God's sheep
Prophecy	Ability to know future events with 100% accuracy; or to speak God's Word with power	1 Cor. 12:10, 28, 29; 14:1-40; Eph. 4:11	Speaking timely messages in the power of God's Spirit
Teaching	Ability to clearly present the truths of Scripture so that they are understood	Rom. 12:7; 1 Cor. 12:28, 29	Clarifies and explains God's Word in an understandable way
Word of knowledge	Ability to share extraordinary knowledge about God & his Word	1 Cor. 12:8	Focuses on & shares from depths of God's Word
Word of wisdom	Ability to share a message applying God's wisdom to the situation	1 Cor. 12:8	Focuses on practicality of Bible & gives good advice

QUESTIONS FOR GROUP DISCUSSION

Orientation/First Meeting

If you are providing books for the group, you may want to meet an extra week to build community and discuss your schedule.

The leader should begin the time with prayer, followed by a time of sharing. If the group doesn't already know one another, start with some basic personal information and maybe one fun question that can be answered without a dissertation. For example, you can ask about a favorite home, vacation, book, or movie. Then use the discussion questions below.

Group Discussion
- How would you define leadership?
- What person has been most spiritually influential in your life?
- Where are you currently influencing someone else?
- What do you hope to accomplish through the study of this book?

What to prepare before the next meeting:
- Read the Introduction.
- Read Chapter 1. Wait to complete the Personal Action Plan until after your next meeting.

Tips for small group success:
- Build community through good discussion, personal sharing, and prayer.
- Give out a schedule the first week so that everyone knows meeting dates and what to read and prepare in advance.
- Start and end on time.
- Keep your group small enough for good interaction and community.

- Have a designated leader who takes initiative and willingly leads the group through the discussion and prayer time.
- Follow-up is important. Find a volunteer to send out a weekly email with everyone's prayer requests on it within 24 hours. The leader may want to send an email reminding everyone of what to prepare for the next meeting and sharing her enthusiasm for the group.
- Consider the discussion questions listed each week, but feel free to tailor them to your specific group and their needs. Enjoy the interaction.

Chapter 1 Discussion: The Fragrance of Leadership

Group Discussion

+ Do you relate to any aspect of Kay's story in the Introduction? How?
+ What scares you about being a leader, or what makes you hesitant to exert spiritual influence?
+ How does wearing the label of "leader" make you feel?
+ From the various definitions of leaders, which ones do you like best? Why?
+ Discuss the elements you consider necessary to the fragrance of leadership.
+ Share the definitions of leadership which you wrote.
+ Read Matt. 28:18-20; Titus 2:3-5; 1Peter 4:10-11 and discuss the ways we are to exert spiritual influence. In which area of influence do you need to accept responsibility to lead others? Which area describes leadership that you are already living out?

Prayer Time

End your meeting by praying in groups of three or four if you have a group of six or more. Share two requests per person: the first should be personal to you or your family; the second should be a request for God to expand your leadership in a particular way. Instead of talking about them, write your requests on a card to pass to the next woman who will pray for them by reading the card. After class, a volunteer can take the cards and email the requests to the group.

Before the next meeting:

+ Complete the Personal Action Plan for Chapter 1. (The leader should spend a few minutes introducing these by looking at this first one as a group this week. She should stress the importance of processing the chapters in this way so that the study results in real growth as a leader.)
+ Read Chapter 2.

Chapter 2 Discussion: Strengthening your Core

Sharing Personal Action Plans

The women can partner to discuss their answers to the Personal Action Plan for Chapter 1, sharing the results of their assessments, planned challenges, and anticipated sources of support. Afterward, one or two women might volunteer to communicate their Personal Action Plans with the larger group.

Group Discussion

+ Do you agree with J. Oswald Sanders's quote at the beginning of the chapter? Why or why not? How have you seen its reality?
+ Read John 15:4-5. Do you have regular spiritual check-ups? What exactly do you do in order to discover where you are spiritually? Do you have an accountability partner or prayer partner? Do you spend time in specific scriptures? What works best for you?
+ Do you ever find yourself mostly talking to God instead of listening to him? Do you tend to tell him what to do rather than seek his will? What makes it so difficult to listen?
+ Were any of these spiritual disciplines new to you? Which ones?
+ What spiritual disciplines have been most helpful to your relationship with God? Why?
+ What spiritual disciplines are most difficult for you? Why?
+ Do you ever struggle with prayer? In what ways have you learned to overcome your problems?
+ Were any of the suggestions in the book helpful to you? Did you try any this week? Do you plan to try any?

Prayer Time

In groups of three or four, discuss one prayer request from each woman and consider how God's will in the situation might be different than yours. Discuss ways to reword the requests, submitting them to God's will. Pray the requests.

Before the next meeting:

+ Complete the Personal Action Plan for Chapter 2.
+ Read Chapter 3.

Chapter 3 Discussion: Dirty Laundry

Sharing Personal Action Plans

Pair up to discuss the answers to the Personal Action Plan for Chapter 2. It would be great for at least one person to share her plan with the larger group.

Group Discussion

- Andrew Seidel suggests that our character is more important than our skills. Would you agree? Why or why not?
- Have you personally watched a leader be ineffective because of character issues? Share the story.
- How difficult is it for you to publically confess your sins and errors? Why? How can believing 1 John 1:9 and James 5:16 help? (Read them.)
- Discuss Teresa of Avila's quote, "Be gentle to all and stern with yourself." Why is this so difficult?
- Have each woman share one story of how God has made her more like Jesus using one of the following: the Spirit, the Bible, trials, or discipline.
- What biblical characters other than Jesus exemplify servant leadership? As a group share specific examples of that person's actions that mark him or her as a servant-leader.
- Discuss specific ways in which a leader might exhibit servanthood today.

Prayer Time

End your meeting confessing and praying for each other. You can pair up or confess to the entire group. Consider sins that are opposite the fruit of the Spirit (Gal. 5:22-23). Think about situations where you lack contentment or faith.

Before the next meeting:

- Complete the Personal Action Plan for Chapter 3.
- Read Chapter 4.

Chapter 4 Discussion: Take the Wind with You

Sharing Personal Action Plans
Using partners, discuss the Personal Action Plan for Chapter 3. Then have at least one woman share her plan with the larger group.

Group Discussion
+ Discuss the meaning of calling or mission as explained at the beginning of the chapter. Talk about the differences in a personal calling and God's call on all believers.
+ Have a volunteer read the two quotes from Os Guinness and Richard Nelson Bolles. Then ask, "In what ways do Christians put secondary purposes before our call to relationship with God?"
+ Refer to the section "Don't Confuse your Calling!" Ask whether anyone has been confused about her mission in these ways.
+ Read 1 Cor. 12:4-11 and discuss the basics about spiritual gifts. You might look at the chart in the Appendix together.
+ Share how one or more of the guidelines for discovering your spiritual gifts helped you find your gifts, if you already know what they are.
+ Have each woman share one aspect of her divine design—spiritual gifting, personality traits, strengths, weaknesses, physical abilities, creative gifts, etc.
+ Share a situation where you felt that you took the wind with you—or one where you didn't.

Prayer Time
Share two requests with your partner: first, a request for yourself or your immediate family, and, second, a request concerning your calling. You may want clarity on your spiritual gifts or a place of service that fits your calling.

Before the next meeting:
+ Complete the Personal Action Plan for Chapter 4.
+ Read Chapter 5.

Chapter 5 Discussion: Do I Have to Go to Africa?

Sharing Personal Action Plans
Discuss the Personal Action Plan for Chapter 4 as partners. Afterwards, allow everyone to share what spiritual gifts she has, knowing they are given by grace rather than merit.

Group Discussion
+ Note that calling is clear where divine design, burdens, and opportunities meet. Discuss burdens the women have identified.
+ Let each woman share how she has been helped in recognizing her calling by one of the following: spiritual markers, life's seasons, seeing God at work, or prioritizing God's kingdom.
+ Discuss Luke 4:42-43, John 17:4, and 2 Tim. 4:6-8. How do the examples of Jesus and Paul help you recognize that you should focus on your calling?
+ Which of the hindrances to focusing on mission are issues for you?
+ Discuss the idea that following your call will make your life out of balance.
+ Ask if anyone has tried to write a mission statement yet. Discuss the process and encourage the group to the point that all of them will attempt to write one in the Personal Action Plan. Discuss any questions they have.

Prayer Time
Share with your partner where you are in finding your calling and writing a mission statement. Pray for God to clarify and to give grace to focus on your calling instead of being distracted by the hindrances. Be specific as you pray for God to open doors of ministry in those areas that match your calling.

Before the next meeting:
+ Complete the Personal Action Plan for Chapter 5.
+ Read Chapter 6.

Chapter 6 Discussion: Baa! Baa!

Sharing Personal Action Plans

Use partners to discuss the answers to the Personal Action Plan for Chapter 5. Ask one or two women to share theirs with the larger group.

Group Discussion

+ Discuss the needs of real sheep. See if anyone in the group has firsthand knowledge of sheep or shepherding to share.
+ Review the biblical images used to picture God's care: shepherd, father, mother, gardener, husband. Which is your favorite? Why?
+ How have those who have influenced you shown care and love? How did it impact the amount of influence they had on you?
+ Read John 10:1-18. How does Jesus' example as the Good Shepherd challenge you to care for those in your circle of influence?
+ What have you learned from experience about accepting others, especially those who haven't trusted Christ yet?
+ How have you provided for the physical needs of those whom you lead?
+ What are your reactions to Mary and Jody's stories of reaching out to others, even taking them into their homes? What do you find positive and negative about their decisions?
+ Have you ever helped provide emotional healing for someone who is in pain? If so, what did you learn that might help others in similar situations?
+ How do you feel about confronting someone whom you love and know well when she needs protection, even from herself?
+ How are you encouraged as you consider ways of entrusting those under your care to the Good Shepherd?

Prayer Time

Work with your partner to write a kingdom prayer for yourself concerning a situation in your life right now. Then write a kingdom prayer for someone close to you who is dealing with a difficulty. Pray for both requests.

Before the next meeting:

+ Complete the Personal Action Plan for Chapter 6.
+ Read Chapter 7.

Chapter 7 Discussion: The Mind's Eye

Sharing Personal Action Plans
Pair up to discuss the answers to the Personal Action Plan for Chapter 6, and have at least one person share her plan with the group.

Group Discussion
+ Discuss the definitions of vision by Bill Hybels and Andy Stanley. Do you prefer one over the other? Why?
+ Explain the difference between calling (mission) and vision.
+ Read Neh. 1:1-2:8 and discuss how God showed him a vision of rebuilding the walls of Jerusalem.
+ Has God ever revealed to you a dream of something he wants to do in similar ways?
+ How crucial would you say the communication of the vision is to its fulfillment? Why?
+ Read Neh. 2:3-5, 11-18 and discuss his example of casting vision.
+ What person or group do you hope to spiritually influence? What are your hopes for her or their future? This week you will work on a way to communicate it in your Personal Action Plan.
+ Have you seen a vision fail because the leader never bought into it? Share the story with the group.
+ Do you have a dream of what God wants to do in your own life? As that vision leaks, how do you remind yourself of it so that you persevere?

Prayer Time
Share with a partner the hardest part of vision casting for you—seeing the vision or communicating it. Pray for one another to grow in the weak area.

Before the next meeting:
+ Complete the Personal Action Plan for Chapter 7.
+ Read Chapter 8.

Chapter 8 Discussion: Having the Know-How

Sharing Personal Action Plans

Use partners to discuss the Personal Action Plan for Chapter 7, and then have someone share her plan with the larger group.

Group Discussion

- Read John Maxwell's quote at the top of Chapter 8. Have you ever had an incompetent leader? What was the result?
- Discuss the two levels of competence needed by a leader.
- How have you discovered the skills and knowledge needed in a new position? Did you ask someone who trained you? Did you read about it? Did you find yourself lost?
- When you realized that you lacked needed skills or knowledge, where did you find help to improve?
- What competencies did you decide that you need in your present role of influence?
- What suggestions for avenues of growth do you have for others who need to learn leadership skills?
- Read Mark 3:14-15. Discuss Jesus' leadership training program.
- Have you benefitted from a mentor/coach? Describe your experience.
- In what areas of your spiritual leadership would a mentor/coach be helpful to you now?

Prayer Time

Discuss with a partner the possibility of recruiting a mentor/coach. Talk about the benefits and about any reluctance that you have. Pray for clarity about your areas of weakness and for guidance as to where to best receive help.

Before the next meeting:

- Complete the Personal Action Plan for Chapter 8.
- Read the Conclusion.
- Complete the Personal Action Plan for the Conclusion

Conclusion Discussion: Moving Beyond Ordinary

Sharing Personal Action Plans

Share the Personal Action Plan for Chapter 8 with a partner. Save discussion of the final Personal Action Plan for the end of the discussion.

Group Discussion

+ How do you feel about being a spiritual influence/leader after studying this book?
+ Which of the six fundamentals of leadership has most stirred you? Why?
+ Of the six fundamentals, which two do you expect to work on most during this next year? What is your plan?
+ Have you already implemented any of the fundamentals in your relationships with those whom you hope to lead spiritually? If so, share what you have done.
+ Have each woman share her answers to these questions from her Personal Action Plan:
    o How do you plan to continue challenging yourself as a leader?
    o Where do you plan to get ongoing support?
+ As each one answers, ask another woman to pray for her according to what she shared.

Spend the rest of your time celebrating what God has done as you have worked through the six fundamentals of leadership.

Suggested Resources

Centered in Christ

Spiritual Disciplines in General
Barton, Ruth Haley. *Invitation to Solitude and Silence: Experiencing God's Transforming Presence*. Downers Grove, IL: Intervarsity Press, 2004.

———. *Sacred Rhythms: Arranging our Lives for Spiritual Transformation*. Downers Grove, IL: IVP Books, 2006.

Buchanan, Mark. *The Rest of God: Restoring your Soul by Restoring Sabbath*. Nashville, TN: Thomas Nelson, 2006.

Calhoun, Adele Ahlberg. *Spiritual Disciplines Handbook: Practices that Transform Us*. Downers Grove, IL: IVP Books, 2005.

Foster, Richard J. *Celebration of Discipline: The Path to Spiritual Growth* (20th anniversary edition). San Francisco, CA: HarperSanFrancisco, 1998.

———. *Prayer: Finding the Heart's True Home*. New York: HarperOne, 1992.

Willard, Dallas. *The Spirit of the Disciplines: Understanding how God Changes Lives*. New York: HarperOne, 1991.

Lectio Divina
Petersen, Eugene H. *Eat This Book: A Conversation in the Art of Spiritual Reading*. Grand Rapids, MI: William B. Eerdmans Publishing Co., 2006.

Reinhold, Judge and Amy, eds. *Be Still and Know that I Am God: 31 Days to a Deeper Meditative Prayer Life*. New York: Howard Books, 2007.

Bible Study
Arthur, Kay, David Arthur, and Pete DeLacy. *The New How to Study your Bible: Discover the Life-Changing Approach to God's Word*. Eugene, OR: Harvest House Publishers, 2010.

Hendricks, Howard G., and William D. Hendricks. *Living by the Book*. Chicago, IL: Moody Press, 2007.

Character
Bridges, Jerry. *The Practice of Godliness*. Colorado Springs, CO: NavPress, 2006.

Sanders, J. Oswald. *Spiritual Leadership: A Commitment to Excellence for Every Believer.* Chicago, IL: Moody Press, 2007.

Willard, Dallas. *Renovation of the Heart: Putting On the Character of Christ.* Colorado Springs, CO: NavPress, 2002.

Calling

Resources to help you discover your divine design.

Bolles, Richard Nelson. *How to Find Your Mission in Life.* Berkeley, CA: Ten Speed Press, 2005.

*Brazelton, Katie. *Pathway to Purpose for Women: Connecting your To-do list, your Passions, and God's Purposes for your Life.* Grand Rapids, MI: Zondervan, 2005.

Flynn, Leslie. *Nineteen Gifts of the Spirit.* David C. Cook Communications, 1994.

Jones, Laurie Beth. *The Path: Creating Your Own Mission Statement for Work and for Life.* New York: Hyperion, 1996.

*Miller, Arthur F., Jr. *The Power of Uniqueness: How to Become Who You Really Are.* Grand Rapids, MI: Zondervan, 2002.

Care

Haugk, Kenneth C. *Don't Sing Songs to a Heavy Heart: How to Relate to Those who are Suffering.* St. Louis, MO: Stephen Ministries, 2004.

Hislop, Beverly White. *Shepherding a Woman's Heart: A New Model for Effective Ministry to Women.* Chicago: IL: Moody Publishers, 2003.

———. *Shepherding Women in Pain: Real Women, Real Issues, and What you Need to Know to Truly Help.* Chicago, IL: Moody Publishers, 2010.

Communicating Vision

Blackaby, Henry T., and Claude W. King. *Experiencing God: Knowing and Doing the Will of God.* Nashville, TN: Lifeway Press, 2007.

Hybels, Bill. *Axiom: Powerful Leadership Proverbs.* Grand Rapids, MI: Zondervan, 2008.

———. *Courageous Leadership.* Grand Rapids, MI: Zondervan, 2002.

Stanley, Andy. *Making Vision Stick.* Grand Rapids, MI: Zondervan, 2007.

———. *Visioneering: God's Blueprint for Developing and Maintaining Vision.* Sisters, OR: Multnomah Publishers, 1999.

Competence

Administrative Leadership

Ellis, Lee. *Leading Talents, Leading Teams: Aligning People, Passions and Positions for Maximum Performance.* Chicago, IL: Northfield Publishing, 2003.

Gangel, Kenneth O. *Feeding and Leading: Practical Handbook on Administration in Churches and Christian Organizations.* Grand Rapids, MI: Baker Books, 2000.

Westing, Harold J. *Church Staff Handbook: How to Build an Effective Ministry Team,* 2nd ed. Grand Rapids, MI: Kregel Publications, 1997.

Bible Study Leadership

Arthur, Kay, David Arthur, and Pete DeLacy. *The New How to Study your Bible: Discover the Life-Changing Approach to God's Word*. Eugene, OR: Harvest House Publishers, 2010.

Belenky, Mary Field, Blythe McVicker Clinchy, Nancy Rule Goldberger, and Jill Mattuck Tarule. *Women's Ways of Knowing: The Development of Self, Voice, and Mind*. 10th anniversary ed. New York: Basic Books, 1997.

Gangel, Kenneth and Howard G. Hendricks, eds. *The Christian Educator's Handbook on Teaching: A Comprehensive Resource on the Distinctiveness of True Christian Teaching*. Grand Rapids, MI: Baker Books, 1988.

McBride, Neal F. *How to Lead Small Groups*. Colorado Springs, CO: NavPress, 1990.

Yount, William R. *Called to Teach: An Introduction to the Ministry of Teaching*. Nashville, TN: Broadman & Holman Publishers, 1999.

———. *Created to Learn: A Christian Teacher's Introduction to Educational Psychology*. Nashville, TN: Broadman & Holman Publishers, 1996.

Dealing with Conflict

Edwards, Sue G. and Kelley M. Mathews. *Leading Women who Wound: Strategies for an Effective Ministry*. Chicago, IL: Moody Publishers, 2009.

Sande, Ken. *The Peacemaker: A Biblical Guide to Resolving Personal Conflict*. Grand Rapids, MI: Baker Books, 2004.

General Resources on Leadership

Barna, George, ed. *Leaders on Leadership: Wisdom, Advice and Encouragement on the Art of Leading God's People*. Ventura, CA: Regal, 1997.

Engstrom, Ted. *The Making of a Christian Leader: How to Develop Management and Human Relations Skills*. Grand Rapids, MI: Zondervan Publishing House, 1976.

Seidel, Andrew. *Charting a Bold Course: Training Leaders for 21st Century Ministry*. Chicago, IL: Moody Publishers, 2003.

NOTES

Chapter 1

1. Linda Clark, ed., *5 Leadership Essentials for Women: Developing Your Ability to Make Things Happen* (Birmingham, AL: New Hope Publishers, 2004), 9.
2. "Topic: Leadership," http://www.quoteland.com/topic.asp?CATEGORY_ID=91 (accessed Nov. 15, 2010).
3. Dwight D. Eisenhower, "Topic: Leadership," http://www.quoteland.com/topic.asp?CATEGORY_ID=91 (accessed Nov. 15, 2010).
4. Ted Engstrom, *The Making of a Christian Leader: How to Develop Management and Human Relations Skills* (Grand Rapids, MI: Zondervan Publishing House, 1976), 20.
5. J. Oswald Sanders, *Spiritual Leadership: Principles of Excellence for Every Believer* (Chicago, IL: Moody Press, 1994), 27.
6. Fred Smith, *Learning to Lead* (Waco, TX: Word, 1986), 117.
7. J. Robert Clinton and Richard W. Clinton, "The Life Cycle of a Leader," in *Leaders on Leadership: Wisdom, Advice and Encouragement on the Art of Leading God's People*, ed. George Barna, (Ventura, CA: Regal, 1997), 162.
8. Quoted by George Barna "Nothing is More Important than Leadership," in *Leaders on Leadership: Wisdom, Advice and Encouragement on the Art of Leading God's People*, ed. George Barna (Ventura, CA: Regal, 1997), 21.
9. George Barna, "Nothing is More Important than Leadership," in *Leaders on Leadership: Wisdom, Advice and Encouragement on the Art of Leading God's People*, ed. George (Ventura, CA: Regal, 1997), 21.
10. John C. Maxwell, *Leadership 101: What Every Leader Needs to Know* (Nashville, TN: Thomas Nelson Publishers, 2002), 61.
11. Caye Cook, e-mail to the author, Aug. 18, 2011.
12. Jack Hayford, "The Character of a Leader" in *Leaders on Leadership: Wisdom, Advice and Encouragement on the Art of Leading God's People*, ed. George Barna (Ventura, CA: Regal, 1997), 65.
13. Maxwell, *Leadership 101*, 13.
14. Chris Brady, "Launching a Leadership Revolution," Women's Ally: Don't Just Work, Work Your Career, http://www.womensally.com/articles/Launching-Leadership-Revolution (accessed Nov. 15, 2010).

15 Sanders, *Spiritual Leadership*, 48.
16 Eds. Cynthia D. McCauley, Ellen Van Velsor, *The Center for Creative Leadership Handbook of Leadership Development*, 2nd ed. (San Francisco, CA: Jossey-Bass, 2004), 3.
17 Sanders, *Spiritual Leadership*, 107.
18 Ibid.

Chapter 2
19 Sanders, *Spiritual Leadership*, 18.
20 Jeff Iorg, *The Character of Leadership: Nine Qualities that Define Great Leaders* (Nashville, TN: B&H Publishing Group, 2007), 160.
21 Sanders, *Spiritual Leadership*, 94.
22 See the Appendix for a partial list.
23 Richard J. Foster, *Prayer: Finding the Heart's True Home* (New York: HarperOne, 1992), 13.
24 Ibid., 3.
25 See my article "Kingdom Prayers" at http://bible.org/seriespage/kingdom-prayers (accessed May 12, 2012).
26 Ruth Haley Barton, *Sacred Rhythms: Arranging our Lives for Spiritual Transformation* (Downers Grove, IL: IVP Books, 2006), 32.
27 Dallas Willard, *The Spirit of the Disciplines: Understanding how God Changes Lives* (New York: HarperOne, 1991), 163.
28 Mark Buchanan, *The Rest of God: Restoring your Soul by Restoring Sabbath* (Nashville, TN: Thomas Nelson, 2006), 3.
29 Buchanan, *The Rest of God*, 126.
30 Willard, *Spirit of the Disciplines*, 166.
31 Dr. Gail Seidel, e-mail message to author, Nov. 12, 2010.
32 Foster, *Prayer*, 149.
33 Adele Ahlberg Calhoun, *Spiritual Disciplines Handbook: Practices that Transform Us* (Downers Grove, IL: IVP Books, 2005), 167.
34 Eugene H. Petersen, *Eat This Book: A Conversation in the Art of Spiritual Reading* (Grand Rapids, MI: William B. Eerdmans Publishing Co., 2006), 91.
35 Calhoun, *Spiritual Disciplines Handbook*, 164.
36 See the book written by staff of Precept Ministries on inductive Bible study: Kay Arthur, David Arthur, and Pete DeLacy, *The New How to Study your Bible: Discover the Life-Changing Approach to God's Word* (Eugene, OR: Harvest House Publishers, 2010).
37 Jan Winebrenner, *Intimate Faith: A Woman's Guide to the Spiritual Disciplines* (New York: Warner Books, 2003), 47.
38 Calhoun, *Spiritual Disciplines Handbook*, 176.
39 Ibid., 74.
40 Kay Spinelli, e-mail message to author, Oct. 19, 2010.

Chapter 3

41   Andrew Seidel. *Charting a Bold Course: Training Leaders for 21ˢᵗ Century Ministry* (Chicago: Moody Publishers, 2003), 35.

42   Dwight L. Moody at http://www.quoteland.com/author/Dwight-L-Moody-Quotes/6602/ (accessed May 12, 2012).

43   Oswald Chambers at http://www.quoteland.com/author/Oswald-Chambers-Quotes/2146/(accessed May 12, 2012).

44   Thomas Paine at http://www.quoteland.com/author/Thomas-Paine-Quotes/344/ (accessed May 12, 2012).

45   Teresa of Avila at http://www.quoteland.com/author/Teresa-of-Avila-Quotes/1401/ (accessed May 12, 2012).

46   Dallas Willard, *Renovation of the Heart: Putting On the Character of Christ* (Colorado Springs, CO: NavPress, 2002), 15.

47   Sarah Young, *Jesus Calling: Enjoying Peace in His Presence* (Nashville, TN: Thomas Nelson, 2004), 12.

48   Jennifer Radabaugh, e-mail message to author, Nov. 4, 2010.

49   Evelyn Christenson, *Lord, Change Me!* (n.p: Evelyn Christenson Ministry, 2008.)

50   Willard, *Renovation of the Heart*, 23.

51   Calvin Miller, *The Empowered Leader: Ten Keys to Servant Leadership* (Nashville, TN: Broadman & Holman Publishers, 1995), 16-17.

52   Engstrom, *Making of a Christian Leader*, 19.

53   Iorg, *Character of Leadership*, 117.

Chapter 4

54   Os Guinness, *The Call: Finding and Fulfilling the Central Purpose of Your Life* (Nashville, TN: Word Publishing, 1998), 47.

55   Ibid., 43.

56   Richard Nelson Bolles, *How to Find Your Mission in Life* (Berkeley, CA: Ten Speed Press, 2005), 19.

57   *O: The Oprah Magazine*, Nov. 2010, 170-185.

58   MOPS is the acronym for Mothers of Preschoolers, the ministry of MOPS International.

59   Sanders, *Spiritual Leadership*, 83.

60   Vickie Kraft, e-mail message to author, October 12, 2010.

Chapter 5

61   Tullian Tchividjian, "Our Calling, Our Spheres," posted 9/06/2010 on www.christianitytoday.com/le/.

62   Henry T. Blackaby and Claude W. King, *Experiencing God: Knowing and Doing the Will of God* (Nashville, TN: Lifeway Press, 2007), 123-127.

63   Inductive Bible study material available from Precept Ministries International, Chattanooga, TN at www.precept.org.

64 Susie Hawkins, e-mail to author, Oct. 28, 2010.

65 Katie Brazelton, *Pathway to Purpose for Women: Connecting your To-do List, your Passions, and God's Purposes for your Life* (Grand Rapids, MI: Zondervan, 2005), 186.

66 Laurie Beth Jones, *The Path: Creating Your Own Mission Statement for Work and for Life* (New York: Hyperion, 1996), 63.

Chapter 6

67 Timothy S. Laniak, *While Shepherds Watch their Flocks: Forty Daily Reflections on Biblical Leadership* (China: ShepherdLeader Publications, 2007), 36.

68 "Sheep: Behavior and Intelligence," Wikimedia Foundation, http://en.wikipedia.org/wiki/Sheep#Behavior_and_intelligence (accessed Nov. 18, 2010).

69 Laniak, *While Shepherds Watch*, 17.

70 Patrick L. Townsend and Joan E. Gebhardt, *Five-Star Leadership: The Art and Strategy of Creating Leaders at Every Level* (New York: John Wiley & Sons, Inc., 1997), 64.

71 Carmen Renee Berry, "In Search of Spiritual Community" in *Leadership Journal* (Fall 2003), 12.

72 Ibid.

73 M. Gay Hubbard, *Women: The Misunderstood Majority: Overcoming Myths that Hold Women Back* (Dallas: Word Publishing, 1992), 165-173.

74 Berry, "In Search of Spiritual Community," 12.

75 Laniak, *While Shepherds Watch*, 255.

76 MOPS is the acronym for Mothers of Preschoolers, the ministry of MOPS International.

77 Nancy Fowler, e-mail message to author, March 10, 2011.

78 Ibid.

79 W. Phillip Keller, *A Shepherd Looks at Psalm 23* (Grand Rapids, MI: Zondervan, 2007), 140.

80 Mary Anderwald, e-mail message to author, March 15, 2011.

81 Jody Curran, e-mail message to author, March 24, 2011.

82 Beverly White Hislop, *Shepherding a Woman's Heart: A New Model for Effective Ministry to Women* (Chicago, IL: Moody Publishers, 2003), 154.

83 Anonymous, e-mail message to author, April 4, 2011.

84 See my article "Kingdom Prayers" at http://bible.org/seriespage/kingdom-prayers (accessed May 12, 2012).

Chapter 7

85 Bill Hybels, *Axiom: Powerful Leadership Proverbs* (Grand Rapids, MI: Zondervan, 2008), 30.

86 Andy Stanley, *Visioneering: God's Blueprint for Developing and Maintaining Vision* (Sisters, OR: Multnomah Publishers, 1999), 18.

87 Bill Hybels, *Courageous Leadership* (Grand Rapids, MI: Zondervan, 2002), 31.

88 Kenneth O. Gangel, "What Leaders Do," in *Leaders on Leadership: Wisdom,*

    Advice and Encouragement on the Art of Leading God's People, ed. George Barna (Venture, CA: Regal, 1997), 41.

89 Bill Hybels, *Holy Discontent: Fueling the Fire that Ignites Personal Vision* (Grand Rapids, MI: Zondervan, 2007), 25.

90 Hybels, *Courageous Leadership,* 38.

91 George Barna, "The Vision Thing," *Leaders on Leadership: Wisdom, Advice and Encouragement on the Art of Leading God's People,* ed. George Barna (Venture, CA: Regal, 1997), 52.

92 For more information go to www.titus2-4.com.

93 Stanley, *Visioneering,* 85.

94 Based on Andy Stanley's list in *Making Vision Stick* (Grand Rapids, MI: Zondervan, 2007), 86.

95 Hybels, *Axiom,* 17.

96 Stanley, *Making Vision Stick,* 18.

97 Jody Curran, e-mail message to author, Mar. 24, 2011.

98 Ibid.

99 Mary DeMuth, e-mail message to author, Sept. 27, 2010.

100 Patsy Bolin, e-mail messages to author, Oct. 20, 2010.

101 Hybels, *Courageous Leadership,* 36.

102 Ibid., 44.

103 Stanley, *Making Vision Stick,* 15.

Chapter 8

104 John C. Maxwell, *The 21 Indispensable Qualities of a Leader* (Nashville, TN: Thomas Nelson, 1999), 30.

105 Information about Precept Ministries International, Chattanooga, TN, can be found at www.precept.org.

106 Claudia explains this quote: "Basically, it means that it is my job to teach; whether that is Bible Study, leadership development skills, etc., and I am responsible for how I teach. Am I preparing well? Is it truth? Is it presented in an understandable format? But, I can't learn it for someone else. It is the student's responsibility to take what is taught (either by teaching, what is read in a book, or heard in a workshop or in the Bible) and actually apply it, do it, live it. That is the learning part. I can't learn you. Only you can learn from what is taught." (Claudia McGuire, e-mail message to author, July 20, 2011).

107 Claudia McGuire, e-mail message to author, July 19, 2011.

Conclusion

108 Sue Edwards, e-mail message to author, June 23, 2011.

ABOUT THE AUTHOR

Kay Daigle's mission is to teach God's Word, train godly leaders, and give vision and simplicity to ministry so that others are challenged to grow as vessels for God's use in the world. She loves to work with women and desires to equip them as leaders wherever God places them. For more than thirty years, Kay has been ministering to women in a variety of ways: teaching the Bible, holding various leadership positions, speaking to groups of women, and training leadership.

Kay served for a total of ten years on staff at Northwest Bible Church and Prestonwood Baptist Church, both in the Dallas area, leading their women's ministries. She also served over the marriage ministry at Northwest. Kay earned her M.A. in Christian Education with a focus on Women's Ministry from Dallas Theological Seminary and her Doctor of Ministry degree from Gordon-Conwell Seminary in Effective Ministries to Women.

Kay and Gary, both native Texans, have been married for forty years and live in Texas with their two Westies, Libby and Maggie. Their family also includes two adult children, a son-in-law, and a granddaughter.

Kay prefers Tex-Mex over sushi and escargot. She also loves books, movies, and travel, as well as time with good friends.

You can read Kay's personal blog or sign up for her monthly newsletter at www.kaydaigle.com, or you can follow Kay on Twitter @kaydaigle or friend her on Facebook.

Kay's Bible studies are freely available at www.bible.org or her website. In addition, she has written a number of articles posted on bible.org and Faith Village (www.faithvillage.com).